Steck-Vaughn

Reading Comprehension

Building Vocabulary and Meaning

LEVEL

F

Reviewers

Roberta L. Frenkel

Director of English Language Arts
Community School District 3
New York, New York

Kim Winston-Radden

Fourth/Fifth Grade Teacher
MacDowell Elementary School
Detroit Public Schools
Detroit, Michigan

STECK-VAUGHN
A Harcourt Company

www.steck-vaughn.com

ACKNOWLEDGMENTS

Editorial Director Stephanie Muller
Editor Kathleen Wiseman
Assistant Editor Julie M. Smith
Associate Director of Design Cynthia Ellis
Designer Alexandra Corona
Editorial Development Jump Start Press
Design and Production MKR Design, Inc.
Senior Technical Advisor Alan Klemp
Production Coordinator Susan Tyson Fogarasi

Photo Credits: Cover ©George Grall/National Geographic Image Collection; p.2a ©Jeff Divine/Getty Images; p.2b ©Warren Bolster/Getty Images; p.3a ©David Pu'u/CORBIS; p.3b ©Joseph Sohm/CORBIS; p.4a ©Ron Chapple/Getty Images; p.4b ©Jeff Divine/Getty Images; p.4c ©Hulton-Deutsch Collection/CORBIS; p.5a ©Hulton Archive/Getty Images; p.5b,c,d ©Primedia Surfer Archives; p.5e ©Marc Kozai Surfer Archives; p.6 ©Jeff Divine/Getty Images; p.7 ©David Pu'u/CORBIS; p.8 ©Ron Chapple/Getty Images; p.9 ©Warren Bolster/ Getty Images; p.18a ©Lynda Richardson/CORBIS; p.18b ©Franz Lating/Minden Pictures; p.18c ©Jonathan Blair/CORBIS; p.19a ©Stephen Frink/Getty Images; p.19b ©Jeff Hunter/Getty Images; p.20a ©Tui DeRoy/Minden Pictures; p.20b ©Spencer Jones/Getty Images; p.20c ©Lynda Richardson/CORBIS; p.22 ©Mike Severns/Getty Images; p.24 ©Jeff Hunter/Getty Images; p.25 ©David Fleetham/Getty Images; p.34a ©Tom Bean/CORBIS; p.34b ©Gordon Whitten/CORBIS; p.34c ©David Muench/CORBIS; p.34d ©Paul Bennett/CORBIS; p.35a ©David Muench/CORBIS; p.35b ©W. Wayne Lockwood/CORBIS; p.35c ©George H. Huey/Getty Images; p.36a,b ©David Muench/CORBIS; p.37a ©Scott Smith/CORBIS; p.37b ©Bill Ross/CORBIS; p.38a ©Tom Bean/CORBIS; pp.38b,39,40,41 ©David Muench/CORBIS; p.50a ©David W. Hamilton/Getty Images; p.50b ©Natalie Fobes/CORBIS; p.51 ©Norbert Rosing/Getty Images; p.54b,c; 55a,b;56a,b,c;57a,b;58a,b ©William Wegman Photo; p.60 ©Larry Williams/CORBIS; p.64 ©Bettmann/CORBIS; p.70a ©Archivo Iconografico,S.A./CORBIS; p.70b ©Roger Ressmeyer/ CORBIS; pp.70c,71 ©Mimmo Jodice/ CORBIS; p.72a ©Archivo Iconografico,S.A./CORBIS; p.72b ©Mimmo Jodice/CORBIS; p.73a ©Sean Sexton/CORBIS; p.73b ©Mimmo Jodice/CORBIS; p.74 ©Roger Ressmeyer/CORBIS; p.76a ©Mimmo Jodice/CORBIS; p.77 ©Roger Ressmeyer/CORBIS; p.78a ©Keren Su/CORBIS; p.78b ©Charles Krebs/Getty Images; p.78c ©Peter Menzel Photo; p.78d ©Luis Castaneda/Getty Images; p.78e ©Davies & Starr/Getty Images; pp.79a,b;80a ©Peter Menzel Photo; p.80b ©Davis & Starr/Getty Images; p.80c ©Michael Freeman/CORBIS; p.81a ©Peter Menzel Photo; p.81b ©McConnell McNamara/Stock Food; p.81d,e ©Peter Menzel Photo; p.82a ©Davis & Starr/Getty Images; p.82b ©Peter Menzel Photo; pp.82c;83a ©Charles Krebs/ Getty Images; pp.83b; 84a ©Peter Menzel Photo; p.84b ©Charles Krebs/Getty Images; p.84c ©Davies & Starr/Getty Images; p.84e ©Peter Menzel Photo; p.85a ©Charles Krebs/Getty Images; p.85b ©Davies & Starr/Getty Images; p.85d,e ©Peter Menzel Photo; p.94a ©Chris Ryan/Getty Images; p.94b,c ©Hugh Sitton/Getty Images; p.95 ©Keren Su/Getty Images; p.96a ©Angelo Cavalli/Getty Images; p.96b ©Chris Ryan/Getty Images; p.97a ©David Epperson/Getty Images; p.97b ©David Muench/CORBIS; p.97c ©Josef Beck/Getty Images; p.98 ©Kevin Schafer/Getty Images; p.99 ©Hugh Sitton/Getty Images; p.100 ©Keren Su/Getty Images; p.101 ©David Epperson/Getty Images; p.102a ©Max Dannenbaum/Getty Images; p.102b ©Reuters NewMedia Inc./ CORBIS; p.103 ©Max Dannenbaum/ Getty Images; p.106 ©David W.Hamilton/Getty Images; p.107 ©Chris Howes/Getty Images; p.109 ©Chris Ryan/Getty Images; p.110 ©Josef Beck/Getty Images.

Additional photography by Getty Royalty Free.

Illustration Credits: Sue Carlson: p. 21; Cathy Diefendorf: pp. 104, 105; Lane Dupont: pp. 10-17; Brad Gaber: pp. 86-92; Gershom Griffith: pp. 42-49, 52; Barbara Kiwak: pp. 62-69; Geoffrey McCormack: pp. 34-36; Rémy Simard: pp. 26—33.

ISBN 0-7398-5825-4

Printed in the United States of America
6 7 8 9 10 B 08 07

Contents

LESSON 1

Let's Go SURFING!

What Do You Already Know?

What do you know about surfing? Would you ever want to try surfing? Why or why not?

Get Ready to Read

Authors organize articles around the most important idea, or the **main idea**. They use **supporting details** to give additional information about the main idea. As you read, look for the main idea and supporting details in each section.

VOCABULARY

envelop (en VEL uhp) To cover or surround something completely

maneuver (muh NOO vuhr) To move or steer something carefully into a particular position

cresting (KREST ing) Reaching the highest point

Imagine yourself a hundred yards from a glittering sandy beach. Brilliant sunshine fills a crystal clear sky and warms your back. Light dances off the water that surrounds you. You're racing toward the shore at close to 50 miles (80.5 kilometers) per hour. There is only a thin board beneath your feet to separate you from the powerful ocean. A towering wave threatens to **envelop** you, but you stay just ahead of it. Shifting your weight from one foot to the other, you **maneuver** the board through the smooth water below the **cresting** wave. You're surfing!

Tip

You can often find the **main idea** of a paragraph in the first or last sentence.

a surfer paddling to catch a wave

Riding the Waves

Surfing is a water sport performed mostly in the ocean, although some committed surfers try to find waves in large lakes. Surfers use rigid boards to glide across the smooth sloping parts of waves. First, they lie on the boards to paddle out beyond the breaking waves. Then surfers turn to face the beach. Next, they kneel on the boards. Finally, they stand as the wave begins to rise. Surfers ride the wave toward the shore, **prolonging** the ride by moving across the face of the wave.

Skilled surfers use balance and timing to perform an **array** of different tricks. Today's surfers show their skills in two main ways. One type of surfer participates in organized competitions. Judges rank tricks, length of ride, and even grace while riding. This competitive surfing has been accepted by the International Olympic Committee.

Another type of surfer views the sport as a purely personal way to get close to nature. These surfers avoid the competition **circuit** and search the globe for the perfect wave to enjoy in private. You may not be able to admire these surfers' moves in competition, but you can often find videos or magazines that showcase their skills.

VOCABULARY

prolonging (proh LAWNG ing) Making something last longer

array (uh RAY) A large selection or number of things

circuit (SUR kit) A group of related events that people attend

Tip

Find the most important idea in each paragraph, state it in your own words, and find the **details** that support it.

Surfer Talk

360: a trick where the surfer does a complete turn

hang ten: a trick where all ten toes rest on the nose of the surfboard

ono: Hawaiian word for "great"

ripping: doing amazing tricks on a wave

wipe out: when a surfer is knocked off of a surfboard by a wave

the zone: area inside or between waves when they are breaking

VOCABULARY

eliminate (ee LIM uh nayt) Get rid of

identity (eye DEN tuh tee) Who a person is

a surfer riding a wave

Duke Kahanamoku

A Royal History

Surfing traces its history to the early Polynesians, including those living in what is now Hawaii. Some experts believe that Hawaiian kings surfed in their religious ceremonies. Others say that both kings and citizens enjoyed surfing as a sport. In any case, early surfing dates back at least to the 15th century. Change came in the 1800s, however, when large numbers of Europeans arrived in Hawaii. Some Europeans did not like the sport and tried to **eliminate** it.

In 1920, however, a young Hawaiian named Duke Kahanamoku helped bring the sport back by founding a surfing club. Duke was no ordinary Hawaiian. He was an Olympic swimming champion, grandson of a high chief, and an accomplished surfer. Duke gained recognition for his sport by traveling as far away as Australia to show off his skills. Surfing also grew in popularity as more and more people visited Hawaii for its sunny weather and lovely beaches. These tourists brought news of surfing back to the mainland.

Then, during the 1950s and 1960s, the **identity** of the surfer began to change. Surfers developed their own language. You could spot surfers by their suntans and the casual clothes they wore. Before long, surf music and movies helped bring surfing style to young people all over the United States.

The Changing Surfboard

The early Hawaiians surfed on wooden boards that were 18 feet (5.5 meters) long. Duke Kahanamoku's boards were 8 to 10 feet (2.4 to 3 meters) long and solid wood. These surfboards were heavy and hard to handle.

However, over time, surfboards improved. In the 1930s, a surfer looking for speed developed a hollow board. The surfer also added a fin to help him guide the board. Even this board still weighed 60 to 70 pounds (27.2 to 31.8 kilograms)!

It wasn't long before lighter woods and plastics led to the *malibu*, a board weighing just 20 pounds (9 kilograms). The *malibu* **transformed** surfing. Now surfers could really steer their boards. They could move around to do tricks. Even carrying a surfboard became much easier. This encouraged surfers to travel in search of "perfect" waves. Most of all, *malibus* made learning to surf easier. This brought more and more people to the sport.

Today's surfboards are very different from those used by the first surfers. The new boards are built mostly of plastic. They are shorter and usually more narrow than the early boards. A typical board is now about 6 feet (1.8 meters) long and weighs about 5 pounds (2.3 kilograms). Also, most boards now have three fins as well as shaped edges to make steering more **precise**. If you ever take to the waves, you'll enjoy these improvements. They'll keep you ahead of that huge wave.

Surfboards Then and Now

	Length	Weight
Before 1930	18 ft.	over 60 pounds (over 27.2 kilograms)
1930s		60–70 pounds (27.2 to 31.8 kilograms)
1960s		20 pounds (9 kilograms)
Today	6 ft.	5–6 pounds (2.3–2.7 kilograms)

Tip

Subheads can suggest the main idea of a section.

Duke Kahanamoku poses with his huge surfboard.

VOCABULARY

transformed (trans FORMD) Made a great change

precise (pree SYSS) Very accurate or exact

Comprehension Check

Circle the letter next to the best answer.

1. What do surfers do after turning to face the beach?

A. Lie on their boards
B. Kneel and stand up
C. Paddle beyond the waves
D. Turn on their video cameras

2. Under which subhead would you most likely find information about surfboards used in the 30s?

E. Riding the Waves
F. The Changing Surfboard
G. Surfer Talk
H. A Royal History

3. In which U.S. city would a surfer most likely live?

A. San Diego, California
B. Dallas, Texas
C. Denver, Colorado
D. Kansas City, Kansas

4. What changed about surfing because of the *malibu*?

E. Competition became tougher
F. Surf clothing became unavailable
G. Surfers could steer better
H. Boards became heavier

Answer the questions below in complete sentences.

5. Identify two basic types of surfers. How are they similar and different?

____

____

____

6. What are two ways that surfing has changed since the 15th century?

____

____

____

Vocabulary Builder

Use the words in the box to complete the paragraph.

circuit
eliminate
envelop
transformed

As the fog begins to ______(1)______ the beach, we can hardly see our way to the shore. When the sun rises, the heat will ______(2)______ the fog and we will feel warmer. By noon, the once quiet beach will be ______(3)______ by a crowd of noisy surfers. The competition ______(4)______ has added our beach to its list.

EXTEND YOUR VOCABULARY

Dictionary Skills **Dictionaries give word spellings to help the reader with pronunciations. They also give definitions of the word.**

Answer the first part of each item by writing a word from the box on the line. Answer the second part by circling the correct choice. Use your glossary to help you.

array	cresting	identity	maneuver	precise	prolonging

5. Write the correct spelling of (KREST ing). ____________
It means— **a.** rising **b.** falling

6. Write the correct spelling of (pree SYSS). ____________
It means— **a.** general **b.** exact

7. Write the correct spelling of (muh NOO vuhr). ____________
It means— **a.** wander **b.** steer

8. Write the correct spelling of (pro LAWNG ing). ____________
It means— **a.** lasting longer **b.** stopping suddenly

9. Write the correct spelling of (uh RAY). ____________
It means— **a.** a selection **b.** just one choice

10. Write the correct spelling of (eye DEN tuh tee). ____________
It means— **a.** who you are **b.** naming someone

Focus Skill

Main Idea and Supporting Details

Writers organize nonfiction articles around a **main idea**. They add **supporting details** to give readers more information.

Choose one section in the article. Fill in the main idea chart by writing the subhead, the main idea, and supporting details.

Main Idea

Subhead ______________________

____

Supporting Detail ______________________

____

Supporting Detail ______________________

____

Use the article and your main idea chart to answer the questions.

1. Which sentence from this section best tells the main idea?

____

2. How do the supporting details help you understand the main idea?

____

____

Your Turn to Write

Choose a sport or activity you know well. Use the main idea chart below to develop a main idea that tells about the topic. Then write some supporting details.

Main Idea ______________________________
____

Supporting Detail ______________________________
____

Supporting Detail ______________________________
____

Supporting Detail ______________________________
____

On a separate sheet of paper, write a short article about your sport or activity. Use the information from your main idea chart.

LESSON 2

LOST!

What Do You Already Know?

Have you ever been hiking or camping? What did you see? What skills did you use?

Get Ready to Read

The **plot** includes all the events in a story. The **rising action** includes the events that lead up to the **climax**, or most exciting part. The **falling action** includes events that lead to the **resolution**, or how the problem is solved. As you read, look for the problem and resolution.

VOCABULARY

anticipation
(an TISS uh pay shuhn) Expecting something to happen and being excited about it

strenuous
(STREN yoo uhs) Needing great energy or effort

Matt was burning with **anticipation**. Today he and his sister Lynn were finally going to scale Canfield Peak. He'd wanted to tackle the climb since he was six years old. Now that Lynn was in college and Matt was in middle school, Matt's mom had agreed that they could make the hike alone.

Matt banged on Lynn's door. "Hey, let's go before the day disappears," he called.

Lynn and Matt drove to the base of Canfield Peak. With their gear on their backs, they began the **strenuous** climb. At first the time flew by, but as they came closer to the peak, the climb became more and more difficult. After about four tough hours, they reached the peak. The sun blazed high in the sky and the hikers were hot, dusty, and exhausted. But the view was worth the hard work. It was absolutely beautiful and they could see for miles around.

"You did it!" exclaimed Lynn with enthusiasm. "You're an awesome hiker, for a 12 year-old."

"What do you mean, for a 12 year-old? I'm a good hiker for any age," **retorted** Matt. "Let's head back down. That took a lot longer than we thought it would."

After stopping for a snack to **refresh** themselves, Lynn and Matt started back down. Lynn pointed out sights they'd overlooked on the way up. Soon, the hikers came to a fork in the trail.

"Which way, Lynn?" asked Matt, looking puzzled.

"This way," said Lynn, pointing to the right. "I'm almost certain Dad and I turned right here when we did this last year."

They hiked on at a steady pace. However, as the sun sank into the mountains and the temperature dropped, the trail became unfamiliar. They hadn't passed another hiker for miles. There were twists, turns, and decisions to be made every hundred yards. They constantly asked each other, "Right or left? Left or right?"

After an hour of wandering and discussing trail options, Lynn had to admit it. They were lost.

"It's late and almost completely dark," worried Lynn aloud. "I don't think we should keep hiking when we can't see properly. We're just getting more and more lost. I even feel as if we're walking up, not down."

"I think you're right," said Matt. "We've got to come up with a plan and use some **survival** skills."

Tip

In the **rising action**, readers learn about the characters and discover the main story problem.

VOCABULARY

retorted (ri TORT ed) Answered quickly and strongly

refresh (ri FRESH) To feel fresh and strong again

survival (suhr VY vuhl) Staying alive

Tip

To find a story's **climax**, or moment of greatest tension, think about where the story's action changes direction.

They traced their steps back to a small cave that was near a clearing they had recently passed. "This might do the trick," Lynn said, **surveying** the cave.

But Matt shook his head. "I don't think we should stay here," he said. "Look at those tracks leading in and out. There could be wild animals living here. We don't want any unexpected visitors in the middle of the night!"

Then Lynn spotted some large rocks just a few feet off the path. The two looked carefully and discovered a sheltered space between one large rock and a smaller one leaning up against it. "It doesn't look like there are any wild animals in here," Lynn said. "But I bet it is large enough for the two of us to sleep in."

"And small enough to trap our body heat," said Matt. "Now let's go find some branches to help keep us warm."

"Wow, Matt, I'm impressed! I never knew that you were so **resourceful**," Lynn marveled.

The two worked together and soon found enough leafy limbs to cover the opening between the rocks. They filled in the cracks with some leaves and small branches, then added some moss for more protection. The wind was becoming fierce, but it was warm and toasty inside their temporary shelter.

"I think we'll be okay without a fire for the night," said Lynn. "Plus, with this wind and all the dry leaves around the area, it would probably cause more harm than good."

"It's really not that bad in here," said Matt. "Let's divide our food and water. And thank Mom for packing such large lunches."

VOCABULARY

surveying
(SUHR vay ing) Looking at a whole scene or situation

resourceful
(ri SORSS fuhl) Knowing how to do what is needed to solve problems

Huddled together under the leaves and branches, the two sang songs to pass the time and keep calm as the sounds of the mountain crept into their shelter. Coyotes howled, owls hooted, and the wind blew the trees, making them creak and moan.

In spite of their fear, they couldn't help but become **drowsy**. They were worn out from the climb and their efforts to make a decent shelter. Matt grabbed the jacket he'd wisely brought along and draped it across his sister and himself. Soon they fell asleep.

When Lynn awoke, it was morning and Matt was outside the shelter. She rubbed her eyes and tried to focus on what he was doing.

"I'm trying to signal for help, Lynn," he said. "I'm using the cap of the metal thermos to reflect the sunlight to the base of the mountain. It works almost like a flashlight."

Watching him in the dawn light, Lynn realized that her baby brother had turned into an **extraordinary** young man. After what seemed like hours, Matt thought he heard some distant calls.

"Hey, Lynn," shouted Matt, "I think the searchers are headed this way. Lend me your incredibly loud voice to answer their calls."

They hollered, "We're over here!" until they grew **hoarse**. Finally, the searchers emerged from the trees, nearly crashing into Lynn and Matt, who ran full tilt with joy and relief. It was their parents!

Tip

To understand a story's **resolution**, ask yourself what happened to the characters and how they solved their problem.

VOCABULARY

drowsy (DROU zee) Sleepy

extraordinary (ek STROR duh NER ee) Very unusual or remarkable

hoarse (HORSS) Having a rough and husky voice

Comprehension Check

Answer the questions below in complete sentences.

1. Why is Matt so excited about climbing Canfield Peak?

____

____

2. How do Matt and Lynn get lost?

____

____

3. Why doesn't Lynn think they should hike down the mountain in the dark?

____

____

4. How did the author suggest that the hikers were not in terrible danger and would probably end up safe at the end of the story?

____

____

____

5. What steps do Matt and Lynn take to secure themselves for the night?

____

____

____

6. What does Lynn realize about her brother from their hiking experience?

____

____

____

Vocabulary Builder

Circle the letter next to the best answer.

1. In this story, *retorted* means

A bragged loudly
B answered quickly
C argued angrily
D teased gently

2. In this story, *refresh* means to

E complete a task again
F go back the way one came
G give strength back to
H clean up

3. In this story, *hoarse* means

A a four-legged mammal
B feeling nervous
C being skilled at hiking
D having a rough voice

4. In this story, *survival* means

E staying alive
F having good study habits
G caring for crops
H hiking and rock climbing

EXTEND YOUR VOCABULARY

Synonyms **Synonyms are words with the same or similar meanings.**

Circle the two words in each row that are synonyms.

5. resourceful	helpless	capable	clumsy
6. easy	interesting	demanding	strenuous
7. injury	drowsy	tired	humor
8. ordinary	remarkable	secret	extraordinary
9. surveying	panicking	looking	taking
10. expectation	determination	communication	anticipation

Focus Skill

The **plot** of a story includes the **rising action**, **climax**, **falling action**, and **resolution**.

Use the information from the story to fill in the plot chart. List story events in the best place along the path.

Climax

____

Problem

____

____

Falling Action

____

____

Rising Action

Matt and Lynn climb

the mountain together.

Resolution

____

____

Use the story and your plot chart to write the answers.

1. Explain your choice for the story's turning point or climax.

____

____

2. How does the story's ending resolve the characters' problem?

____

____

Your Turn to Write

Think of an adventure that you have had. Use the plot chart below to plan a story about that adventure.

Climax

Problem

Falling Action

Rising Action

Resolution

On a separate sheet of paper, write a story about your adventure. Use the information from your plot chart.

LESSON 3

The Long Road Home:

The Life Cycle and Migration of Green Sea Turtles

What Do You Already Know?

Have you ever seen a turtle that lives in the water? What did it look like? How did it move?

sea turtle eggs

VOCABULARY

hatchlings (HACH lings) Baby animals that have come from eggs

hazards (HAZ uhrds) Dangers or risks

encounter (en KOUN tuhr) Meet, especially in a dangerous way

Get Ready to Read

Sequence is the order of events in a story or an article. Authors use sequence to help the reader understand how and when things happen. As you read, think about the sequence of the green sea turtle's life cycle.

Dozens of tiny green sea turtles paw quickly at the sand all around them. They've just hatched from their soft eggs and lie buried in a sandy nest. To survive, they must scratch their way to the surface and crawl to the sea. Working as a group, the baby turtles finally emerge from the nest into the cool night air.

The mother turtle is gone. She left the nest some sixty days earlier after laying the eggs. Now the **hatchlings** face many **hazards** as they struggle to stay alive. First, they must figure out where the sea is. Some scientists think they do this by looking for the brightest horizon. Next, the hatchlings must reach the sea before they dry out in the sun. They also may **encounter** crabs or birds who want to eat them.

Growing Up

Because their mother is gone, baby turtles that reach the ocean will swim unprotected from sharks and other large fish. With such dangers, it takes great effort and **persistence** to reach giant beds of seaweed far offshore. The seaweed offers warm waters, food, and protection from enemies.

Adrift and floating in weeds, the baby turtles spend several years eating and growing. They eat worms, baby crabs, sea insects, and plants. Then they find their way to feeding grounds that are closer to shore. For several more years, the teenaged turtles eat and grow their way toward being full-sized. It can take 20 years or more to become an adult. As a result of many challenges on the road to adulthood, just one in one thousand baby sea turtles actually grows to be an adult turtle.

Most green sea turtle feeding grounds are in warm, coastal waters. Adult turtles spend their days eating sea plants and resting. They sleep beneath the safety of shore rocks.

When fully mature, these green sea turtles may be about 3 feet (.9 meters) long and weigh 300 pounds (136 kilograms). Size and strength will help the turtles **evade** enemies on yet another journey.

Tip

Units of time such as **days** and **years** can help you follow a sequence.

baby sea turtles swimming

VOCABULARY

persistence (puhr SIST uhns) Ability and willingness to keep going in spite of challenges

adrift (uh DRIFT) Drifting or floating freely through water or air

evade (ee VAYD) To keep out of something's way; to avoid

Tip

Phrases that begin with the word **once** can relate the timing of one event to the timing of another.

After laying her eggs, the mother turtle returns to sea.

Journey to the Nest

Every few years, adult green sea turtles swim from their feeding grounds to nesting areas that are far away. When mating time approaches, both male and female turtles begin the long journey back to the nesting site. Amazingly, the turtles can **navigate** their way to very specific nesting sites, often the same site where they themselves were born. Some green sea turtles, for example, feed and spend much of their adult lives on the coasts of South America. But they lay their eggs on Ascension (uh SEN shuhn) Island far out in the Atlantic Ocean. To get to the nesting area, the turtles must make a journey of nearly 1400 miles (2200 kilometers).

Scientists are not certain how sea turtles find their way when they travel such long distances. One new theory suggests that turtles can sense the magnetic forces from the North and South Poles. By sensing these forces, the turtles determine where the nesting sites are on the globe.

Once they reach the nesting grounds, mating begins in the waters near shore. When they are ready to lay their eggs, the females head to shore. Night often shields the green sea turtles from predators as they climb the beach. Each female turtle has her own favorite spot that she returns to again and again.

In a dry area safe from the surf, the mother turtle digs a deep nesting hole. It is **oblong**, shaped a bit like a drop of water with a wider than usual tip. She then begins to deposit her eggs. She lays two or three at a time, a total of 80 to 120 eggs, deep into the pit. Finally, she covers the nest with sand. She may return to the same spot four or five more times that season to lay more eggs. Then she heads back to her feeding ground to begin the cycle again.

VOCABULARY

navigate (NAV uh gayt)
To find one's way on or across

oblong (ob LAWNG)
Having an elongated shape

Protecting the Turtles

Green sea turtles are ancient animals. They have been around for millions of years. Today, however, they face a serious danger. Feeding and nesting grounds have been disturbed or destroyed, often by human activities. In some places, other sea turtles are already **extinct**. People are afraid that the green sea turtle may follow.

One way to protect green sea turtles is to learn more about them, their habits, and how they have changed over the years. The best way to find out about green sea turtles of long ago is by looking at their **fossils**. To find out about the behavior of the turtles today, scientists can study their patterns of migration. They place small metal tags on female turtles at their nesting sites. They can track the turtles' paths by reading the tags at feeding sites or even by finding lost tags. Scientists also use space satellites to track turtles. The satellites locate signals sent by tracking devices that are attached to the turtles.

Ordinary people can do their part to protect green sea turtles and other animals, too. One way is to keep the world's beaches and oceans clean. Studies show that many turtles die from accidentally eating plastic and other garbage found on or near beaches. Another way to protect the sea turtles is to keep their nesting grounds safe so hatchlings have a greater chance of survival. Finally, people can work together to prevent illegal hunting of the turtles for their meat and shells. Through these efforts, green sea turtles will hopefully be around for a long time to come.

Tip

Time signal words such as **again**, **then**, and **finally** show sequence.

Scientists can use satellites to track the path of a sea turtle.

VOCABULARY

extinct (ek STINGKT) No longer living or existing

fossils (FOSS uhls) Remains or traces of plants or animals from the past

Comprehension Check

Fill in the circle next to the best answer.

1. Baby sea turtles get out of their nest—

Ⓐ by being carried on top of their mothers' backs
Ⓑ by working as a group to dig out
Ⓒ when wind blows the nest open
Ⓓ with help from their fathers

2. Very few baby sea turtles become adult turtles because—

Ⓔ the babies don't try very hard
Ⓕ their fathers sometimes eat them
Ⓖ they face many dangers on land and sea
Ⓗ the mother turtle does not lay very many eggs

3. Where do green sea turtles nest?

Ⓐ In warm, coastal waters
Ⓑ In a dry area safe from the surf
Ⓒ Beneath the safety of shore rocks
Ⓓ On giant beds of seaweed far out to sea

4. Which of the following makes the *best* title for this article?

Ⓔ Human Threats to Green Turtles
Ⓕ Ascension Island's Turtles
Ⓖ Animal Migration Habits
Ⓗ Green Sea Turtles, from Birth to Nesting

Answer the questions below in complete sentences.

5. How do you know that an adult green sea turtle is strong?

____

____

____

6. Why has it become especially important for scientists to learn about sea turtles?

____

____

____

Vocabulary Builder

Circle the best meaning for each underlined word.

1. Sea turtles might become <u>extinct</u> if harm is done to their environment.

   larger in number — died out — hunted for food

2. It takes great <u>persistence</u> for scientists to learn about sea turtles.

   amounts of money — intelligence — energy and effort

3. Scientists may <u>encounter</u> problems such as lost identity tags.

   face — create — report

4. Baby turtles can spend years <u>adrift</u> in the ocean.

   buried — floating — nesting

5. No one is sure how the sea turtles <u>navigate</u> the vast ocean.

   drift on — float across — find their way across

6. Beach garbage is one of the many <u>hazards</u> that baby turtles must face.

   food sources — hiding places — dangers

7. Scientists study <u>fossils</u> to learn about sea turtles from long ago.

   animal remains — newly hatched eggs — migration paths

EXTEND YOUR VOCABULARY

Analogies **An analogy compares two pairs of words. The second pair of words must have the same relationship as the first pair of words.**

Complete each analogy below with a word from the box.

evade	hatchlings	oblong

8. *Frog eggs* are to *tadpoles* as *turtle eggs* are to ________________.

9. *Journey* is to *voyage* as *escape* is to ________________.

10. *Sea turtle* is to *green turtle* as *shape* is to ________________.

Focus Skill

Sequence

Sequence is the order in which events happen. Writers use clue words to help readers follow the sequence in the correct order.

Use the information from the article to fill in the sequence chart. Tell the sequence of events in a green sea turtle's life.

First

The baby sea turtle hatches from an egg buried in the sand.

Next

____

Then

____

Finally

____

Use the article and your sequence chart to write the answers.

1. What is the first thing that baby turtles do after hatching from their eggs?

____

____

2. Name two steps in the sea turtle nesting sequence in the correct order.

____

____

Your Turn to Write

Think about something that grows and changes, such as a plant or an animal. What are the steps in its life cycle? Use the sequence chart below to record the sequence of events.

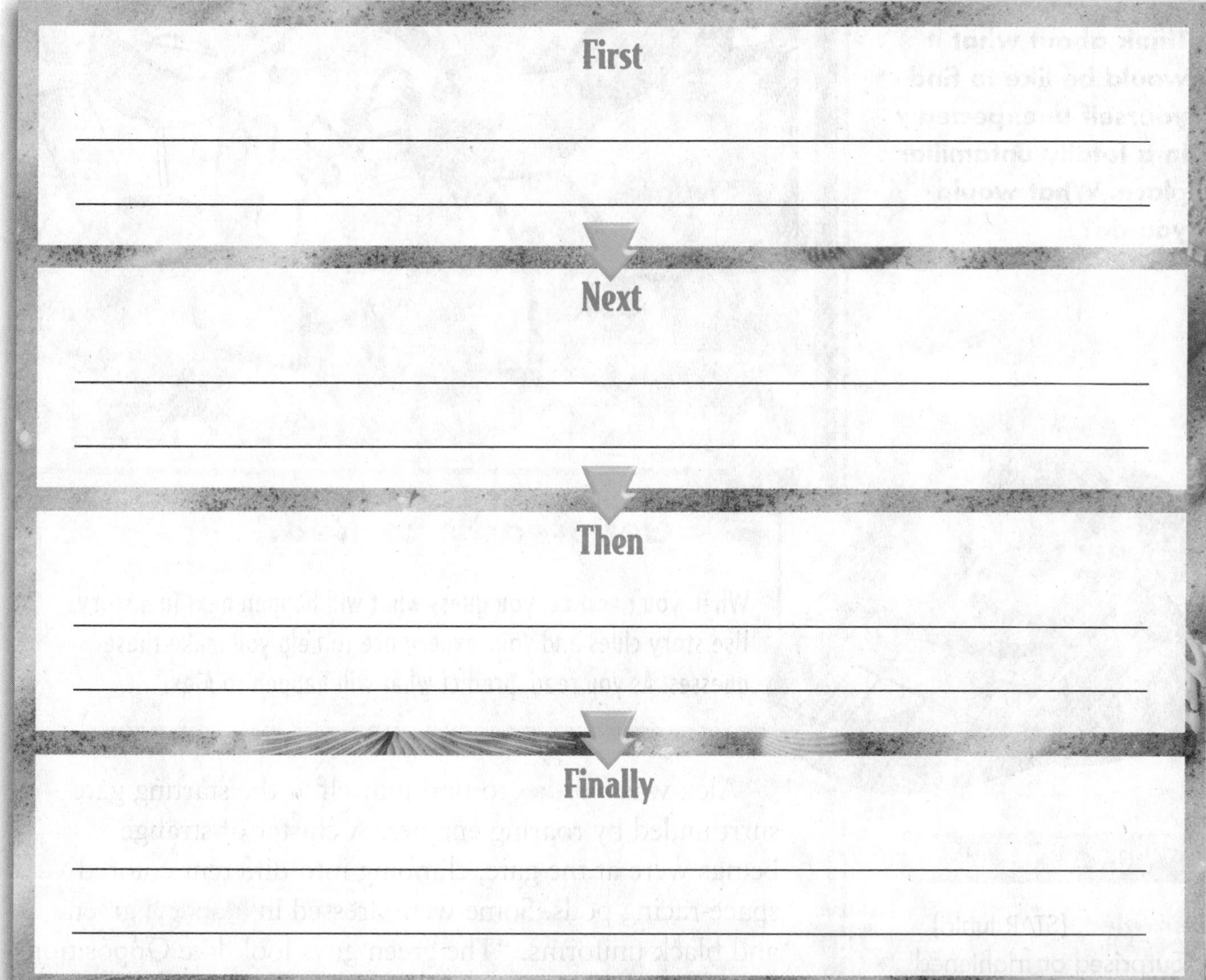

On a separate sheet of paper, write an article about the life cycle of something that grows and changes. Use the information from your sequence chart.

LESSON 4

What Do You Already Know?

Think about what it would be like to find yourself unexpectedly in a totally unfamiliar place. What would you do?

Space Racer 2: It's More Than a Game!

Get Ready to Read

When you **predict**, you guess what will happen next in a story. Use story clues and your experience to help you make these guesses. As you read, predict what will happen to Alex.

VOCABULARY

startled (STAR tuhld) Surprised or frightened

identical (eye DEN ti kuhl) Exactly alike

sinister (SIN is tuhr) Evil and threatening

Alex was **startled** to find himself at the starting gate surrounded by roaring engines. A cluster of strange beings were at the gate, climbing into different colored space-racing pods. Some were dressed in **identical** green and black uniforms. "The green guys look like Opposition Racers from *Space Racer 2*," Alex said. Then he looked down and realized that he was wearing the blue and white uniform of an officer from his favorite video game.

Holding his gloved hands in front of his face, Alex gasped, "Am I really here? Am I inside *Space Racer 2*? Why am I not getting ready for school?"

Suddenly, Alex noticed the Opposition Racers flashing him **sinister** looks that made his skin crawl.

Alex turned away and focused on the space-racing pod awaiting him in the left track entrance area. The pod was a beauty. It was gleaming blue and white in the strange greenish light.

Now I know exactly where I am, thought Alex. *I've played this game every day for a month, but I always crash and burn on this level.* Alex felt his heart leap. "It doesn't matter. I'm going to **demolish** these guys," Alex said. No matter how he'd landed in this other world, Alex loved to race and was determined to win.

For the next few minutes, all the racers worked steadily on their pods. The Opposition Team continued to look suspiciously at Alex, moving to block his view of their work. He wondered what they were up to. Finally, a voice reached Alex through his mind-to-mind communication system. "Five minute warning. Please complete final checks and start your engines."

Alex took a last look at his pod's racer bars and thruster rockets before climbing into the driver's **enclosure**. He buckled himself in. Then he examined the different functions on his instrument board. "What do you suppose this *Defense Action* button is? They don't have this on *my* version of the game," Alex wondered aloud. "Let's hope I won't need that, whatever it is," he said as he pushed a button to start the engine. The roar was deafening.

Tip

Pay attention to how characters act toward one another. This can give you **clues** about what might **happen next**.

VOCABULARY

demolish (di MOL ish) To destroy; defeat badly

enclosure (en KLOH zuhr) An area closed off by walls

Tip

Thinking about what **you know** can help you predict. Put yourself in the same situation as a character, then **imagine** what might happen next.

Just ten feet away, the Opposition Racers were loading the driver into his enclosure. The driver turned to his teammates and cackled.

"Just wait until the second lap and then I'll get him. This guy isn't going to steal the honor we deserve," he said, pushing his helmet down over his head.

"Yeah, boss," replied one racer. "This guy from the real world doesn't stand a chance," she said, chuckling wickedly as she strode to the viewing stand.

The numbers on Alex's panel counted down 10, 9, 8, 7, 6, and so on. At 1, he thrust the bar forward and felt the pod **accelerate** with a lunge.

For the first lap, Alex kept his eyes glued to the race track and tried to ignore his competition. He carved the shortest possible track with his pod—Alex really wanted to win this race. At the end of one lap, Alex glanced for an instant toward the next track. The Opposition Racer was ahead, but only by the length of a pod. Alex was certain he could take the lead in the next lap.

Meanwhile, the Opposition driver shouted into his communication system, "Get ready, I'm going to let him have it." The driver pushed the red button carefully hidden under his seat and streams of space garbage, including meteorites, **ejected** from his pod toward Alex's track.

VOCABULARY

accelerate
(ak SEL uhr ayt) To go faster and faster

ejected (ee JEK tuhd)
Pushed out

All of a sudden, Alex's pod began **careening** from left to right. "What's going on?" he shouted. "I can't drive with all this junk in my path."

As he searched for a solution, Alex saw his opponent's face. It was twisted with evil excitement. Alex realized the Opposition had rigged the race by dumping this **debris** in his path! Alex was **outraged**. He growled through his clenched jaw, "I'm not giving up so easily."

Sweat poured off Alex's upper lip as he tried to concentrate on the track ahead. His pod headed for the stadium wall. "I'm out of control!" he screamed.

Just then an alarm sounded—a familiar alarm. He also heard a familiar voice on his mind-to-mind communication system. It sounded like . . . his mother? Suddenly, he felt the pod start to shake violently. He screamed again, "I'm breaking up!"

"Wake up," said Alex's mother as she shook her son. "You're having a bad dream."

Alex shrugged himself awake. "Wow, Mom, I dreamt I was a pod racer in *Space Racer 2*. I was just about to crash. You know I should have used that *Defense Action* button," he added.

"I think you need to spend a little less time playing that game!" chuckled his mom.

"Or," Alex said with a sparkle in his eye, "a little more!"

Tip

When you get to the end of a story, think about what **could** happen to the characters after the story.

VOCABULARY

careening (kuh REEN ing) Swaying from side to side while moving quickly; lurching

debris (duh BREE) The scattered pieces of something; rubbish

outraged (OUT rayjd) Extremely angered

Comprehension Check

Answer the questions below in complete sentences.

1. What is the setting of this story?

2. Which parts of this story could actually happen and which parts could not?

3. How does Alex feel about taking part in the space race?

4. What kind of beings are the Opposition Racers? How can you tell?

5. What is the mood in the story as Alex struggles to control his pod? How does this mood affect readers?

6. Why does Alex think that his space-racing pod is breaking up? What is really happening?

Vocabulary Builder

Circle the letter next to the best answer.

1. In this story, identical means—

A. very familiar
B. green and black
C. totally different
D. exactly the same

2. In this story, debris means—

E. scattered pieces; rubbish
F. steering wheels; car parts
G. space-racer pods
H. directions; instructions

3. In this story, demolish means—

A. deposit
B. decrease
C. defeat
D. deny

4. In this story, enclosure means—

E. open area
F. closed area
G. clothes rack
H. end of a race

5. In this story, sinister means—

A. evil
B. kind
C. fast
D. glare

6. In this story, outraged means—

E. exhausted
F. angered
G. demanded
H. defeated

EXTEND YOUR VOCABULARY

Context Clues **When you see an unfamiliar word, read the words around it to figure out the meaning.**

Write the word that best completes each sentence.

accelerate	careening	ejected	startled

7. Alex was ________________ to find himself inside a video game.

8. He was suddenly ________________ around corners in a racing pod.

9. Alex pushed the bar forward to ________________ the speed.

10. He hoped he would not be ________________ from the driver's seat.

Focus Skill

Predict

When you **predict**, look for clues that suggest how characters may act or how events may unfold. When you find new clues, use them to adjust your predictions.

Complete the prediction chart. Use details from the story that gave clues about what happened at the end.

My Prediction

Alex will discover that he is only dreaming.

Story Clues That Helped Me Predict

Answer the questions below in complete sentences.

1. As you read the story, was there a prediction you made that you had to change? What new information led you to change it?

2. Do you think Alex will continue to play video games so much? Explain.

Your Turn to Write

Suppose Alex's dream had not ended when it did. What do you think would have happened next? Use clues from the story to make a prediction for a new ending. Write your ideas in the prediction chart below.

My Prediction

____

Story Clues That Helped Me Predict

____

____

____

____

On a separate sheet of paper, write a new story ending about what happens as Alex continues the race. Use the information from your prediction chart to write your ending.

LESSON 5

Rock On!

Incredible Rock Formations

What Do You Already Know?

Have you ever seen strange-looking rock formations like the ones shown here? How do you think the rocks got their shapes?

Pinnacles National Monument

Get Ready to Read

Writers **compare** to show how two or more things are alike. They **contrast** to show how the things are different. As you read, look for ways rock formations are alike and ways they are different.

You're standing beneath what looks like a 1200-foot (360-meter) rock needle. Columns of rugged rocks tower above you. Have you landed on Mars? No, you're at Pinnacles National Monument in California.

These unusual rock towers were created in part by erosion where water wore away the rock, helping to create these fantastic forms. As millions of years **elapsed**, rock canyons, columns, arches, and other shapes appeared.

Pinnacles is just one of the places in the United States where you can find these amazing formations. Capitol Reef National Park and Arches National Park also have **intriguing** rock formations.

VOCABULARY

elapsed (ee LAPSD)
Passed, usually referring to time

intriguing (in TREEG ing)
Fascinating; interesting

Capitol Reef National Park

Utah

Arches National Park

Capitol Reef National Park

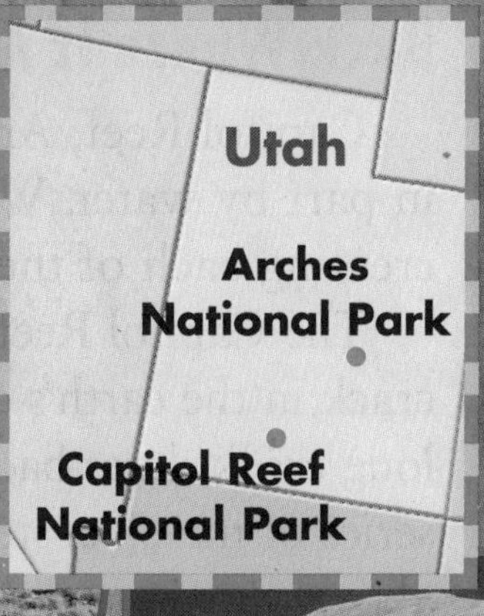

Tip

Look for words and phrases such as **however**, **in contrast**, and **unlike** to help you locate contrasts.

Arches National Park

Where in the World?

Tourists from all over the world come to visit the amazing rock formations found in U.S. national parks. Many can be found in the southwestern part of the U.S.

Capitol Reef is in south-central Utah. It is the second largest national park in the state. Arches National Park is a smaller park found in Utah, near the city of Moab. Pinnacles, however, lies far away in California, south of San Francisco.

If you go to visit Capitol Reef and Arches, be sure to pack your sunscreen and light clothing! The climates around both these areas have **scorching** heat during the day and little rain. In these two parks, you'll only see **sparse** desert vegetation.

In contrast, the climate of Pinnacles in northern California is less dry. Pinnacles also features more plant and animal variety. If you hike through the park, keep your eyes peeled for deer, foxes, and various birds.

Much of the beauty of all of these parks can be viewed from a car. Some of the land in these parks, however, is **accessible** only by foot. For example, you must walk if you want to see the world famous Landscape Arch at Arches National Park.

VOCABULARY

scorching (SKORCH ing) Extremely hot

sparse (SPARSS) Thinly spread

accessible (ak SESS uh buhl) Reachable

Landscape Arch, Arches National Park

Tip

Words such as **all**, **like**, and **also** signal comparisons.

How Waterpocket Fold Was Formed

VOCABULARY

adjacent (uh JAY suhnt) Close to or next to

molten (MOHLT uhn) Melted by heat

Back Where It All Began

Capitol Reef, Arches, and Pinnacles were all formed in part by water. What other factors played a role in creating each of these natural wonders?

The Capitol Reef formations began with an ancient crack in the earth's crust. This 100-mile (161-kilometer) long crack dates back 50–70 million years. It created a series of massive, steep cliffs 7000 feet (2133.6 meters) above the **adjacent** land. It is now called the Waterpocket Fold. Water erosion left large pockets that give the fold its name.

Sandstone played a major role in shaping the rocks at both Capitol Reef and Arches. Sandstone is unusually soft and more easily eroded than most other types of rock. At Arches National Park, wind, rain, and frost carved the arch formations in sandstone that are more than 80 million years old.

Like Capitol Reef, Pinnacles Monument also began with a crack in the earth's crust, which is now known as the San Andreas fault line. About 30 million years ago, **molten** rock from the earth's core burst up through this crack, forming a volcano. Over time the volcano erupted many times as it grew and grew. Many of the shapes that later became part of Pinnacles Monument were actually formed by burning hot lava! Over time, erosion by water and wind wore down the rocks to what they are today.

Formation of Pinnacles National Monument

Capitol Reef, Capitol Reef Park

Tip

Sometimes the author does not give clue words to show comparisons and contrasts. Pay attention to what each paragraph **describes.**

All Shapes, Sizes, and Colors

The layers of sandstone at Capitol Reef reveal many colors. This area was once called the "Land of the Sleeping Rainbow" by the Navajo because of the brilliantly colored canyon walls. One part of the park, however, is filled with white domes that **adorn** the landscape. They reminded scientists of buildings like the U.S. Capitol, which is how the park got its name. Glass Mountain is also a must-see at Capitol Reef Park. It formed when minerals in water **accumulated** into a giant hill of glassy crystals.

The sandstone in Arches National Park is reddish and has been molded into arches of all sizes. The park includes more than 90 arches. Landscape Arch is the longest in the world at 291 feet (88.7 meters). Delicate Arch is the most famous because it is the Utah state symbol. Other arches are just 3 feet (1 meter) across, which is the **minimum** distance to qualify as an arch. The Fiery Furnace section has rocks shaped like giant fish fins. These tower around canyons like sharks of the desert!

At Pinnacles, needle-like towers rise out of the Gabilan Mountains, east of central California's Salinas Valley. These spectacular remains of an ancient volcano range from 500 to 1200 feet (152 to 366 meters) high. The tallest is the stunning Chalone Peak. Pinnacles is also filled with deep, dark caves.

All of these rock formations offer information about Earth's history, and each offers its own special beauty for visitors to enjoy.

Delicate Arch, Arches National Park

VOCABULARY

adorn (uh DORN)
Decorate

accumulated
(uh KYOOM yoo lay ted)
Collected; piled up

minimum (MIN i muhm)
The smallest possible amount

Comprehension Check

Circle the letter next to the best answer.

1. Which of the following best summarizes the article?

- **A.** Traveling to the American Southwest is interesting.
- **B.** Many interesting rock formations can be found in U.S. national parks.
- **C.** Pinnacles National Monument was formed by a volcano.
- **D.** Water is a major cause of rock erosion.

2. This article is most like a—

- **E.** short story
- **F.** poem
- **G.** magazine article
- **H.** folktale

3. If you wanted to see a variety of wildlife, where would you go?

- **A.** Capitol Reef Park
- **B.** Arches National Park
- **C.** Near the city of Moab, Utah
- **D.** Pinnacles National Monument

4. What happened first to form the Pinnacles National Monument?

- **E.** Molten rock poured up through a crack in the earth's crust.
- **F.** Some shapes were formed by burning hot lava.
- **G.** The volcano erupted many times as it grew and grew.
- **H.** Wind and water erosion created rock formations.

Answer the questions below in complete sentences.

5. How did the Capitol Reef area form?

____

____

____

6. What do you think will happen to the rock formations at Pinnacles, Capitol Reef, and Arches as erosion continues over time?

____

____

____

Vocabulary Builder

Write the words from the box to complete the paragraphs.

accessible	**accumulated**	**adjacent**
elapsed	**intriguing**	**minimum**

Jill and Edward decided to visit Arches National Park. They found the study of rocks ________ (1). Several months ________ (2) while they planned the trip. Finally, the time had arrived!

First they reached the nearby, or ________ (3), town of Moab. They planned to hike to reach the least ________ (4) formations. Edward had ________ (5) a lot of gear in his backpack, including hats and water. They also brought sunscreen with a ________ (6) of 15 SPF to avoid sunburn.

EXTEND YOUR VOCABULARY

Similes **Similes are comparisons between unlike things. When one part of the comparison is familiar to you, you may be able to use it as a clue to the meaning of the unfamiliar part.**

Look at the underlined word and the simile in italic type. Then circle the correct meaning for the underlined word.

7. The desert vegetation was sparse, *like plants in the frozen arctic.*

a. thinly spread b. thick and dense

8. Molten lava flowed slowly down the mountain, *like thick, hot syrup.*

a. crystal rock b. melted by heat

9. Wood burned in the scorching heat, *like fabric under an iron too long.*

a. extreme b. smooth

10. Dome shapes adorn the horizon, *like jewels on a queen's crown.*

a. fill b. decorate

Focus Skill

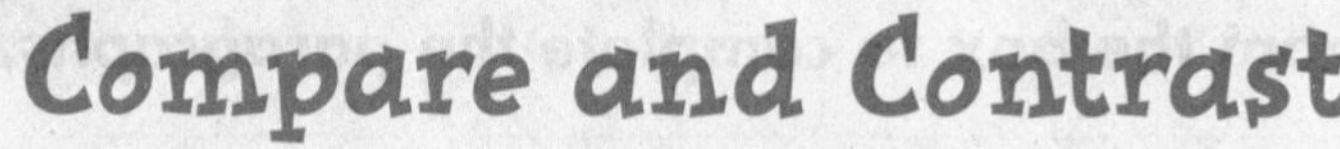

Compare and Contrast

Writers **compare** to show how two or more things are alike. They **contrast** to show how the things are different.

Use the article to fill in the Venn diagram. Under each park's name, write details about that park. Under "Both," write details that tell about both parks.

Pinnacles National Monument	Both	Capitol Reef National Park
located in California	*intriguing rock formations*	*located in Utah*

Use the article and your Venn diagram to write the answers.

1. List one way that all three parks are alike.

____

2. Choose one of the parks. Compare and contrast it to Arches National Park.

____

____

____

Your Turn to Write

Choose two places you know about. Use the Venn diagram below to compare and contrast the two places. Be sure to include details such as where the places are and what they look like.

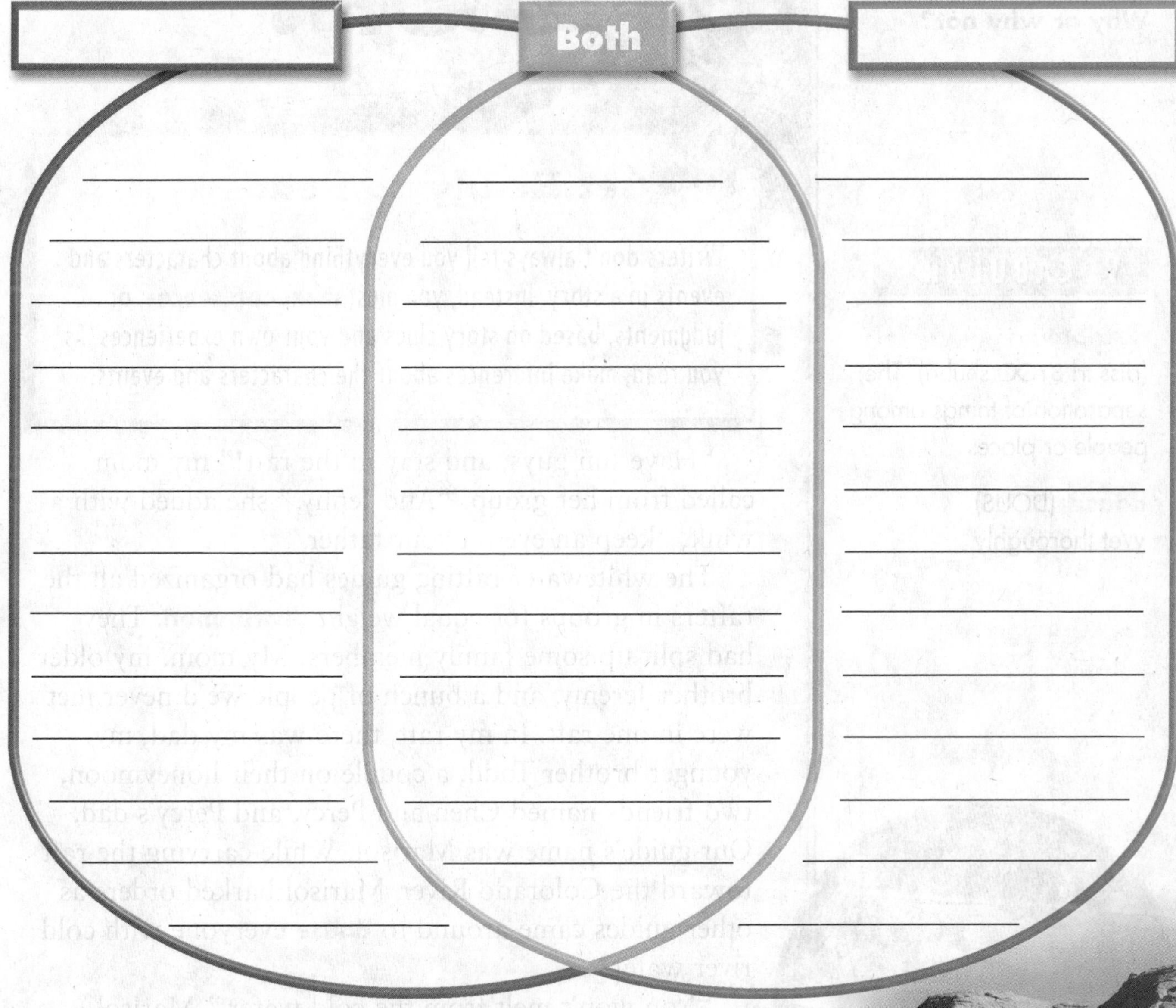

On a separate sheet of paper, write a short article that compares and contrasts your places. Use the information from your Venn diagram to write the article.

LESSON 6

What Do You Already Know?

Have you ever been whitewater rafting? Would you like to try this exciting sport? Why or why not?

VOCABULARY

distribution (diss tri BYOO shuhn) The separation of things among people or places

douse (DOUS) Wet thoroughly

THE BIG SPLASH!

Get Ready to Read

Writers don't always tell you everything about characters and events in a story. Instead, you must **make inferences**, or judgments, based on story clues and your own experiences. As you read, make inferences about the characters and events.

"Have fun guys, and stay in the raft!" my mom called from her group. "And Jenny," she added with a wink, "keep an eye on your father."

The whitewater rafting guides had organized all the rafters in groups for equal weight **distribution**. They had split up some family members. My mom, my older brother Jeremy, and a bunch of people we'd never met were in one raft. In my raft, there was my dad, my younger brother Todd, a couple on their honeymoon, two friends named Chen and Percy, and Percy's dad. Our guide's name was Marisol. While carrying the raft toward the Colorado River, Marisol barked orders as other guides came around to **douse** everyone with cold river water.

"You won't melt from the cold water," Marisol laughed as we yelped with surprise. "Better now than later. You'll have to get used to it. This is a wet ride!"

Everyone cringed at the cold water, but we were determined to act like real rafters. Marisol divided us on the two sides of the raft and demonstrated how to secure ourselves with our feet.

Tip

Your own **experiences** can help you make inferences. Ask yourself why the actions in the story might be necessary or sensible.

"Todd, you'll be stationed back here with me so you can squeeze down all the way into the raft when the going gets rough. That's the safest place for a younger person," Marisol reassured my doubtful dad. "Okay! Are we ready to tackle the rapids?"

Everyone nodded, though I felt pretty **incompetent** about rafting. I glanced repeatedly at Todd, who was perched next to Marisol and had a rope to hold on to because his feet didn't reach the floor. I knew he was a bit nervous, but hoped he'd have fun anyway.

We were off, and quickly felt the raft's **buoyancy** as it hit the river's water and began to float. Our "put-in point" was a stretch of calm, peaceful water that gave us a chance to practice newly learned directions such as "Everyone forward paddle one!" or "Back paddle on the left two, forward on the right three!" At first we had trouble keeping the raft going forward, but soon we caught on and began working like a well-oiled machine.

Our new companion, Percy, pointed to the riverbank where a pair of mountain goats stood silently watching us. Everyone whispered "Wow!" with awe in their voices. The sun blazed hot in the cloudless western sky and I thought to myself how peaceful this seemed. Then, little by little, the raft sped up.

"Paddle! Paddle!" Marisol yelled as we cruised on to rougher waters.

VOCABULARY

incompetent (in KOM puh tuhnt) Not very skilled at something

buoyancy (BOI uhn see) Ability to float

Tip

Think about each character's **mood**. What can you infer from his or her reaction to the situation?

VOCABULARY

frantically (FRAN tik lee) Excitedly

impact (IM pakt) The striking of one thing against another

endanger (en DAYN juhr) To threaten or put in a dangerous situation

"Our first rapid is just ahead," explained Marisol. "It's called 'The Ankle Bone' because we'll travel around a bend in the river shaped like an ankle bone. Everybody remember to paddle on my commands. We need to steer this raft through the rapids. Okay, now everyone check that your feet are secure. Ready . . . forward paddle two!"

I felt my heart rate soar as the sounds of the rapids grew louder and angrier. We all hollered shouts of encouragement as the other rafts plunged into the rapids ahead of us, bucking **frantically** up and down.

When it was our turn, Dad grabbed Todd, and I braced myself for **impact** as the raft headed for the rocks. Water sprayed high into the air around us, splashing us all. Over the rushing noise of the water and the shouts of our group, Marisol calmly instructed us, "Two forward on the left, and now two more." Gradually, the water slowed and the raft settled.

"Awesome!" Todd yelled to me. Rafting had him hooked for sure. "Are there more rapids? Are there more?" he asked Marisol excitedly.

"See," replied Marisol, "you're a river rat after all. Don't worry, you'll get plenty of amazing rides today because the river is high and the water is running fast. But we can't **endanger** your dad, right?" she continued, with a sly grin in my direction.

"I'm ready," I said, hungry for more. "Bring it on." Then I heard more roaring water up ahead.

"Okay folks," shouted Marisol. "This is a big one called 'The Hole,' for obvious reasons. The water wants to suck our raft right down into that hole and we've got to paddle hard to keep on course."

In an instant, it seemed as if we were headed over a **precipice**. The raft dropped down into a narrow stretch of water with steep rocks looming above on all sides. Towering waves crashed all around us as the currents bounced the raft around like a toy. Our raft tipped until it felt like it was almost straight up in the air. I was sure we were about to overturn.

Marisol hollered "High side! High side!" and we all scrambled to weigh down the **teetering** high side. We hung in the air for a moment that felt like a lifetime, and then the raft found its balance again. Once we were stable, Dad grabbed Todd and **embraced** him, asking, "Are you okay? Were you scared?"

"Are you kidding, Dad? This is great, except for you grabbing me every two seconds," he said. I rolled my eyes and grinned at Marisol. We both knew who the scared one was.

As we settled back in our seats, Marisol sounded the call once again. "Paddle! Paddle! Paddle!" she bellowed. I didn't know about my dad, but I was ready for more!

Tip

Pay attention to the characters' **body language**. It can help you make inferences about their personalities and how they are feeling.

VOCABULARY

precipice (PRES uh pis)
A steep cliff

teetering (TEE tuhr ing)
Unstable

embraced (em BRAYSSD)
Clasped; hugged

Comprehension Check

Answer the questions below in complete sentences.

1. What is the reason for dividing up the families among the various rafts?

2. What is the last thing that happens to the rafters before they get into the rafts?

3. From what point of view is this story written? Who is the speaker?

4. What are examples of *dialogue* and of *narration* from the story?

5. What is the climax of this story? Why?

6. How are "The Ankle Bone" and "The Hole" alike and different?

Vocabulary Builder

Circle the letter next to the best answer.

1. In this story, *impact* means—

A effect
B crash
C excitement
D confusion

2. In this story, *precipice* means—

E cliff
F tunnel
G river
H steep

3. In this story, *buoyancy* means—

A largeness
B heaviness
C ability to float
D inability to float

4. In this story, *douse* means—

E dry
F drown
G drip
H drench

EXTEND YOUR VOCABULARY

Antonyms **Antonyms are pairs of words with opposite or nearly opposite meanings.**

Circle the letter next to the antonym for each vocabulary word.

5. frantically	**a.** excitedly	**b.** loudly	**c.** calmly
6. embraced	**a.** released	**b.** clasped	**c.** embarrassed
7. distribution	**a.** collection	**b.** separation	**c.** elevation
8. teetering	**a.** unstable	**b.** stable	**c.** teaching
9. endanger	**a.** risk	**b.** trouble	**c.** secure
10. incompetent	**a.** skilled	**b.** unsuccessful	**c.** include

Focus Skill

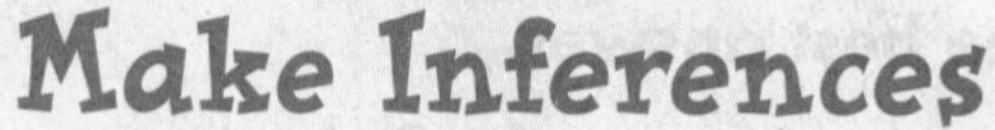

Writers will not always tell you everything about characters and events. You have to **make inferences** about them, using clues and your own experiences.

Use clues from the story and your own experiences to complete the chart and make an inference about Jenny's father.

STORY CLUES

Jenny's mother tells her to look after her father.

____

MY EXPERIENCES

____

____

MY INFERENCE

____

____

Use the story and your chart to answer the questions.

1. Do you think Jenny's family has ever been rafting before? Explain.

____

____

2. How are Jenny's feelings different from her father's feelings?

____

____

Your Turn to Write

Think of a character from a book, movie, or television show. Think about this character's actions or words and your own life experiences. Use the chart to make an inference about this character.

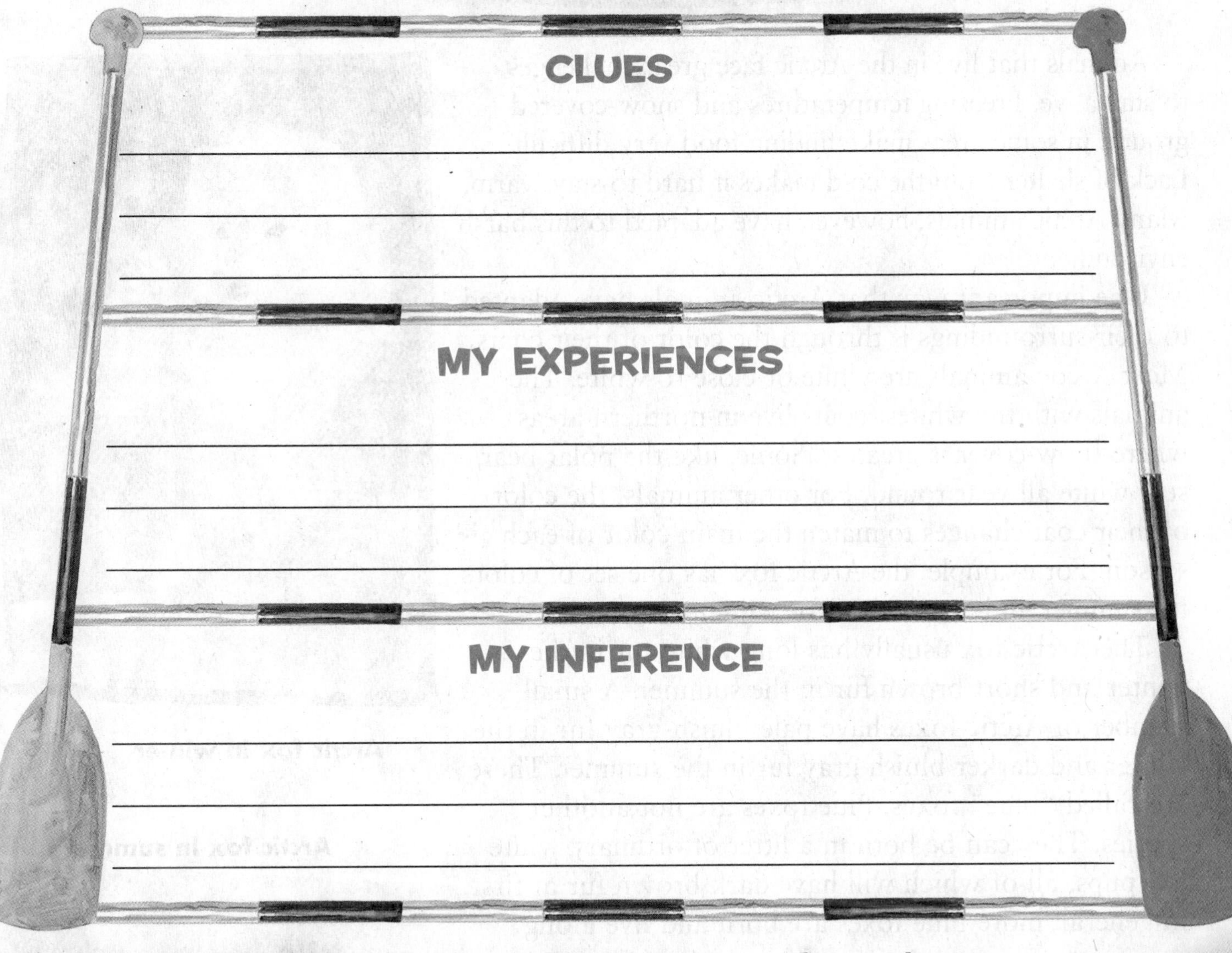

On a separate sheet of paper, write a description of your character. Use the information from your chart.

REVIEW

Read the article. Then answer the questions.

A Coat of Many Colors—Arctic Foxes

Animals that live in the Arctic face great challenges to stay alive. Freezing temperatures and snow-covered ground in some areas make finding food very difficult. Lack of shelter from the cold makes it hard to stay warm. Many Arctic animals, however, have adapted to this harsh environment.

One important way that Arctic animals have adapted to their surroundings is through the color of their coats. Most Arctic animals are white or close to white. The animals with the whitest coats live in northern areas where snow-cover is greatest. Some, like the polar bear, stay white all year round. For other animals, the color of their coat changes to match the main color of each season. For example, the Arctic fox has one set of colors for summer and another set for winter.

Arctic fox in winter

The Arctic fox usually has long white fur in the winter and short brown fur in the summer. A small number of Arctic foxes have pale bluish-gray fur in the winter and darker bluish-gray fur in the summer. These are called "blue" foxes. Blue foxes are not another species. They can be born in a litter of ordinary white fox pups, all of which will have dark brown fur at first. In general, more blue foxes are born and live along coasts where the sea is free of ice much of the winter. These color changes allow the Arctic fox to blend in with its particular surroundings as the seasons change throughout the year. This helps the animal hide itself both as hunter and as hunted.

Arctic fox in summer

Fill in the circle next to the best answer.

1. What color fur do blue foxes have first?

Ⓐ Dark brown
Ⓑ White
Ⓒ Bluish-gray
Ⓓ Pale bluish-gray

2. How is a polar bear's fur similar to that of an Arctic fox?

Ⓔ Both are white only in summer
Ⓕ Both are brown only in winter
Ⓖ Both are white in winter
Ⓗ Both are white all year-round

3. Which would make the best title for this article?

Ⓐ Getting to Know Polar Bears
Ⓑ Comparing Blue and White Foxes
Ⓒ Winter Wonderland
Ⓓ Animals Surviving in the Arctic

4. How are Arctic foxes different in summer than in winter?

Ⓔ In summer they are white and in winter they are blue.
Ⓕ In winter they are brown and in summer they are white.
Ⓖ In summer they are brown and in winter they are white.
Ⓗ In summer and winter they are a mix of white and brown.

Answer the questions below in complete sentences.

5. What is the main idea of this article?

____

____

6. Why might blue foxes be more common along coasts that have little ice?

____

____

7. What might happen if warmer temperatures cause more areas in the Arctic to be free of sea ice?

____

____

____

Read the story. Then answer the questions.

The Final Lap

"Runners, take your marks," blared a voice over the speakers. Kaya pushed the tips of her shoes against the track and then stretched her rear leg into position. Finally, she lowered her body and placed her hands on the track. She closed her eyes and cleared her mind in order to review the race mentally.

This was Kaya's most significant race of the year. Scouts for the Junior Olympic team were observing and she hoped that they'd notice her if she finished in the winner's circle. For Kaya, this win would get her a little closer to her dream of running as a national athlete in the Olympic Games.

Glancing up at the crowd, Kaya caught a thumbs-up from her family. Then she focused on waiting for the final announcement.

"On your marks, get set, GO!" shouted the announcer as Kaya and the other six racers took off like balls out of a cannon. For the first four laps, Kaya worked her way gradually from sixth place to second place. Then she cruised for a short time, gathering strength for the final laps. Her strategy for winning was to outrun the others in the final sprint. It had worked many times before.

As the bell rang for the final lap, Kaya reached deep inside for her remaining energy. She surged forward into the lead, pounding the track with each step and pushing off to lengthen her stride. The crowd rose to its feet as Kaya pulled away from the remaining field of runners and streaked across the finish line.

Circle the letter next to the best answer.

1. What is the first thing Kaya does?

A She lowers her body and places her hands on the track.

B She pushes her shoe tips against the track.

C She runs as fast as she can.

D She stretches her rear leg into position.

2. What is the resolution of the story?

E Kaya grinds her shoes into the dirt.

F Kaya surges forward into the lead.

G The announcer yells, "On your marks, get set, GO!"

H Kaya crosses the finish line.

3. Just before Kaya begins to sprint, she—

A gathers strength by maintaining position for a few laps

B uses all her strength to pull ahead of the other racers

C moves up in position from sixth to second

D races across the finish line

4. What will Kaya probably do next in this story?

E Talk with her coach about why she lost the race.

F Run around the track several more times.

G Receive a first-place ribbon.

H Congratulate the winner.

Answer the questions below in complete sentences.

5. What can you infer about Kaya's previous experiences with racing?

____

____

6. What is the climax, or period of greatest tension, in this story?

____

____

7. Will Kaya reach her goal of running in the Olympics? Explain.

____

____

LESSON 7

WILLIAM WEGMAN: A DOG'S BEST FRIEND

What Do You Already Know?

A biography is the true story of someone's life. Think about famous people you know about. What might their biographies say about them?

Photography Courtesy of William Wegman

Photography Courtesy of William Wegman

VOCABULARY

exhibited (eg ZIB it uhd) Shown to the public

Get Ready to Read

A **summary** is a short statement that tells what an article or story is **mostly about**. A summary should be no more than a few sentences. As you read, look for the most important ideas that would go in a summary of William Wegman's life.

Have you ever taken a photograph? Imagine being a photographer and taking pictures all the time. Perhaps you would take pictures of beautiful places, exotic animals, or even famous people.

If you're anything like William Wegman, though, you might photograph something less traditional—like dogs that have been dressed to look like people! William Wegman is an artist who has made a career of doing just that. His work has been **exhibited** in museums and art galleries all over the world. Since he started photographing his dogs in 1970, he has become quite famous. So have his dogs!

An Artist Gets His Start

William Wegman was born in 1943 in Holyoke, Massachusetts. As a boy, William loved to draw and paint. When he was older, he decided to go to art school. William studied art at the Massachusetts College of Art and at the University of Illinois. There he learned all about painting and drawing.

Soon William finished school. He became a **professor** and taught painting in Wisconsin. During this time, however, he became interested in more **contemporary** ways of making art. He was excited by the **media** of film and photography. William experimented with both.

In 1970, William and his wife, Christine, moved from Wisconsin to California. They decided to get a dog once they had moved to their new home. They had heard that Weimaraners (WY muh RAH nuhrz) were good dogs. They answered a newspaper ad from someone selling Weimaraner puppies. That's when they got their first Weimaraner.

William named his new dog Man Ray after a famous photographer. Soon, he discovered that Man Ray was comfortable in front of the camera. He thought Man Ray would make a good subject for some photographs. Fortunately, he decided to try some of his wacky ideas.

Photography Courtesy of William Wegman

Tip

A summary includes only the **most important** ideas and details. As you read, ask yourself, "What are the most important ideas in this section?"

Photography Courtesy of William Wegman

VOCABULARY

professor (proh FESS uhr) A teacher of the highest rank at a college or university

contemporary (kuhn TEM puh rer ee) Up-to-date; modern

media (MEE dee uh) Ways of expressing or carrying information to people

Photography Courtesy of William Wegman

Tip

Look at the **subheads** in an article to help you summarize the main ideas.

VOCABULARY

collaboration (kuh LAB uh RAY shuhn) Working together to do something

reluctant (ri LUK tuhnt) To be nervous about; to not want to do something

photogenic (foht uh JEN ik) To look very good in photographs

inspired (in SPY urd) To be filled with excitement or ideas about something

New Ideas

In the beginning, William photographed Man Ray doing normal dog activities such as eating, sleeping, and chewing on things. But soon William found that he could put Man Ray in different settings, with different props, to create scenes for his photographs. He also discovered that his dog was an enthusiastic model. An unusual **collaboration** was born between the two of them.

Man Ray was the star of William Wegman's many photographs and videos for twelve years. Then, in 1982, Man Ray died of cancer. William was **reluctant** to photograph dogs again. But in 1986, he began to work with another Weimaraner named Fay Ray. He found that Fay Ray was also **photogenic**.

Fay Ray was the first dog William dressed in human clothing. William was in his studio one day and put Fay on a high stool, which made her look tall like a person. He covered her and the stool with an old dress. He discovered that this made the dog look like a woman standing up. William was **inspired**!

Soon Fay Ray had puppies, one of whom later had her own puppies. Now William had a whole cast of dog models, named Chundo, Crooky, Battina, and Chip, to work with. He photographed and videotaped them wearing many different costumes and playing many different roles. The resulting images were both beautiful and funny. William and his Weimaraners were a big success!

The Artist Today

Today, William Wegman's work is known throughout the world. He has used his dogs to create children's books based on stories such as *Cinderella*, *Little Red Riding Hood*, and *Mother Goose*. He has also designed alphabet cards and has made videos with his well-known pooches. He now **resides** in New York City with his wife, two children, and, of course, his dogs.

Many people wonder if William's dogs are really comfortable being dressed up and photographed. But William is gentle with his dogs. He respects each dog's personality. "Every dog is an individual," he says. "Chundo doesn't like to sit long but is most eager to work... Chip doesn't mind hats. Batty falls asleep while posing with or without costume."

William also says, "Anyone who's watched us work sees that the dogs perform **willingly**. Sometimes they're excited or enthusiastic, but they're not afraid."

Clearly, William Wegman is an unusual kind of artist. He has combined his love for making art with his love for dogs. But it's not all fun and games for William and his Weimaraners. "Despite my silly photographs," he says, "it's serious work and the dogs take it seriously."

Photography Courtesy of William Wegman

Tip

Look for the most important ideas from the **beginning**, **middle**, and **end** of an article.

Photography Courtesy of William Wegman

VOCABULARY

resides (ri ZYDZ) Lives

willingly (WILL ing lee) Ready and eager to help or do what is asked

Comprehension Check

Fill in the circle next to the best answer.

1. Why did William Wegman begin experimenting with photography?

Ⓐ His father was a photographer.
Ⓑ Someone gave him a camera.
Ⓒ He wanted to try new media.
Ⓓ He was tired of painting.

2. Which type of photograph did William Wegman take first?

Ⓔ Man Ray doing ordinary things
Ⓕ Man Ray in wacky costumes
Ⓖ Fay Ray in a dress
Ⓗ Fay Ray playing with other dogs

Photography Courtesy of William Wegman

3. Which of these is a statement of opinion?

Ⓐ As a boy, William loved to draw and paint.
Ⓑ The resulting images were both beautiful and funny.
Ⓒ Today, William Wegman's work is known throughout the world.
Ⓓ William Wegman named his dog after a famous photographer.

4. The author wrote this article to—

Ⓔ inform the reader about Weimaraners
Ⓕ persuade the reader to get a Weimaraner
Ⓖ inform the reader about William Wegman's life
Ⓗ entertain the reader with a story about dogs

Answer the questions below in complete sentences.

5. Do you think William Wegman's dogs mind being photographed? Tell what makes you think so.

____

____

6. How do you think the author feels about William Wegman's photographs? Why?

____

____

____

Vocabulary Builder

Circle the word or phrase that best replaces each underlined word.

1. We went to see the photographs <u>exhibited</u> at the Museum of Modern Art.

taken shown borrowed

2. At first, I was <u>reluctant</u> to go to a museum.

excited nervous happy

3. After seeing the famous photographs, I was totally <u>inspired</u>.

full of ideas talented envious

4. We learned that photography is one of the most popular <u>media</u> used today.

connections hobbies forms of communication

5. We even met one of the photographers who <u>resides</u> in the city.

lives goes to school visits occasionally

6. I now know that I prefer <u>contemporary</u> art to the older paintings.

flashy up-to-date artistic

EXTEND YOUR VOCABULARY

Suffixes **A suffix is a word part added to the end of a word to change its meaning.**

Choose a suffix from the box for each root word. Then write the resulting vocabulary word on the line.

-genic = (to have qualities of)	-tion = (the state of)
-or = (one who does something)	-ly = (to do something by being)

7. profess (to share information) ________________

8. willing (ready and eager) ________________

9. collaborate (working together) ________________

10. photo (photograph) ________________

Focus Skill

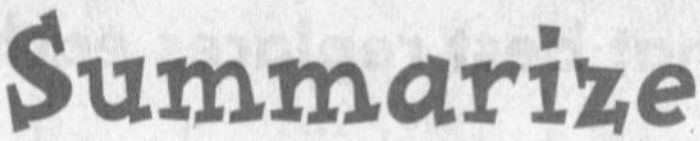

Summarize

When you **summarize** an article or story, you tell the **most important** ideas. Find the most important ideas in each section to help you write a summary.

Use the information from the article to complete the summary chart.

MOST IMPORTANT IDEA OF PAGE 54

William Wegman has made a career of taking photographs of dogs.

MOST IMPORTANT IDEA OF PAGE 55

____

____

MOST IMPORTANT IDEA OF PAGE 56

____

____

MOST IMPORTANT IDEA OF PAGE 57

____

____

Use the article and your summary chart to write the answers.

1. Describe William Wegman's work. Give examples to support your answer.

____

____

2. Why do you think William Wegman has been so successful?

____

____

Your Turn to Write

▶ **Choose someone you admire who has mastered a skill. It could be a famous person, such as an athlete or musician, or it could be someone you know. Use the summary chart below to list important ideas about the person.**

NAME: ____________________

IMPORTANT IDEA

____

____

IMPORTANT IDEA

____

____

IMPORTANT IDEA

____

____

▶ **On a separate sheet of paper, write a summary about the life and achievements of the person you chose. Use the information from your summary chart.**

LESSON 8

A New Land, A New Life

What Do You Already Know?

Have you ever had to do a difficult task by yourself? What challenges did you face? How did you feel?

VOCABULARY

breathtaking
(BRETH tayk ing) Very beautiful or impressive

symbolized
(SIM buh lyzd) Stood for

gangplank
(GANG plangk) A short bridge used for walking onto and off a ship

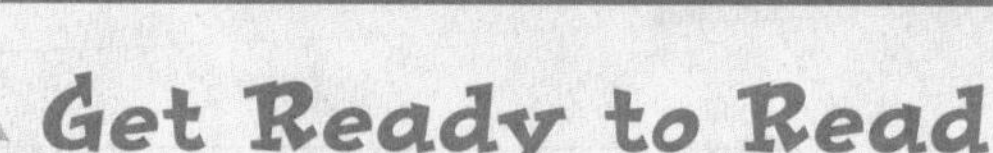

Get Ready to Read

A **character** is a person in a fictional story. You can learn what characters are like from how they think and feel. You can also learn about characters from what they say and do. As you read, look for details that tell you what Malka is like.

Malka stood at the railing of the ship as it pulled into New York Harbor. She gasped at the **breathtaking** sight of the copper statue as it sparkled in the sunlight. To Malka, the sculpture **symbolized** hope for all people, no matter what country they came from.

Malka followed the other passengers down the **gangplank** and onto the crowded dock. After the long ocean journey, she was happy to be on land again. The year was 1900, the dawn of a new century. Malka's heart pounded with fear. Could she survive in this big city after growing up in a tiny village in Russia? Malka had decided she would have to try. She stood tall and walked with determination to greet her new life.

Malka had traveled alone across the ocean to this new land. Her mother, father, two sisters, and brother were back in Russia. Her father was a tailor, but his eyesight had started to fail and he could no longer work. Her mother was forced to support the family. So far, she had made enough money for only one **passage** to America.

"You are the oldest child, Malka," her mother had said. "You will go first and make your way in America. You will live with your Aunt Irina and her family. We will think of you every day, especially when we light the candles on Friday night."

Now Malka thought about her family and she was **overcome** by a wave of sadness. She missed them so much! She longed for them to join her in America. Malka decided at that moment that she must succeed in this new country. She would learn the new language, English, as quickly as she could. She would find work as a **seamstress**. She would work day and night. She would earn enough money to send for her family. Malka would make sure that their **immigration** was easier than her own.

Tip

Descriptions of how a main character feels can tell you what he or she is like. What do Malka's **thoughts** and **feelings** tell you about her?

VOCABULARY

passage (PASS ij)
A journey by ship

overcome
(oh vuhr KUM) To be strongly affected by something

seamstress (SEEM striss)
A woman who sews for a living

immigration
(IM uh gray shuhn) Entry into a new country to live

Tip

Pay attention to the main character's actions. What do Malka's **actions** tell you about what kind of person she is?

Malka and the other passengers filed into the largest room she had ever seen. Malka waited patiently in one line and was given a health test. When she passed that, she was sent to wait in yet another line.

Malka waited as the immigration inspector searched her suitcase. He was looking for **contraband**, items that couldn't be brought into the country. Then he looked at her papers.

"Malka is your Russian name," the inspector boomed. "You are in America now. We will call you Mary." The inspector stamped her papers and Malka was free to go.

With her aunt's address in her hand, Malka hurried out of the building. She smiled as she said the foreign name out loud to herself. *Mary* might be the name on her papers, but she would always be the same in her heart. Her name would always be *Malka*. Outside the large inspection building, a kind man who spoke Russian pointed her in the right direction. Malka walked east across Manhattan Island.

That night, Malka went to sleep in her aunt's apartment in a section of New York called the Lower East Side. The street outside her window was so noisy! At first Malka thought she would never fall asleep, but soon the warmth of the feather bed comforted her and she drifted off to sleep.

VOCABULARY

contraband
(KON truh band) Items not allowed to be brought into another country

Tip

What **other people** say and think about a character can give you clues about what the character is like.

Malka soon learned that the Lower East Side was a neighborhood filled with immigrants from many parts of Eastern Europe. Apartments were crowded, with more than one family living together. Most people were poor and life was very difficult. But people were grateful to be in America. Malka loved her new neighborhood, with its friendly people all struggling together. She also loved the familiar language and foods from her homeland.

Malka found work as a seamstress and worked long hours every day. It was difficult, but Malka **persevered**. She worked hard for many months and saved her money. After awhile, she was able to open a small shop of her own. She mended clothing and made dresses and suits for people in the neighborhood. She worked quickly and charged fair prices. Soon everyone spoke of Malka, the seamstress who made wonderful clothing. Her reputation grew and many people came from other neighborhoods to have their clothing made.

One day a man wearing an expensive suit came into her shop. "I like your designs. I want you to manage my clothing factory," he told Malka. "I will pay you a very good salary."

Malka was so excited. What a **breakthrough**! Her American dream was about to come true. She would soon have enough money to bring her family to her new home.

VOCABULARY

persevered
(pur suh VEERD) Did not give up, even when faced with difficulties

breakthrough
(BRAYK throo) An important step toward achieving something

Comprehension Check

Answer the questions below in complete sentences.

1. Why do you think the author wrote this story?

2. Why did Malka come to America by herself?

3. Why do you think Malka decided not to call herself Mary?

4. Why did Malka work so hard as a seamstress?

5. Why do you think Malka was offered a job managing a clothing factory?

6. What do you think will happen to Malka next?

Vocabulary Builder

Circle the letter next to the best answer.

1. In this story, symbolized means—

- **A** stood up
- **B** sat down
- **C** fell over
- **D** stood for

2. In this story, passage means—

- **E** a long car ride
- **F** a narrow hallway
- **G** a journey by ship
- **H** an exciting tale

3. In this story, seamstress means—

- **A** a man who sews for a living
- **B** a woman who sews for a living
- **C** someone who cooks for a living
- **D** someone who paints for a living

4. In this story, immigration means—

- **E** entry into a new country to live
- **F** going back to one's first country
- **G** traveling around the world
- **H** living in an apartment

5. In this story, contraband means—

- **A** someone who inspects suitcases
- **B** a new name
- **C** thread used by a seamstress
- **D** items not allowed into a country

6. In this story, persevered means—

- **E** felt terrible
- **F** did not give up
- **G** was exhausted
- **H** felt very lonely

EXTEND YOUR VOCABULARY

Compound Words **A compound word is two words joined together to make a new word.**

Underline the compound word in each sentence. Circle the two words within it. Then write the definition of the compound word.

7. Malka was overcome by the sight of the Statue of Liberty.

____

8. As she walked down the gangplank, Malka felt relieved.

____

9. Malka thought the big city was breathtaking.

____

10. She had a breakthrough when the man offered her a job.

____

Character

A **character** is a person in a fictional story. Think about what characters do, say, and think to find out what they are like.

▶ **Use the information from the story to fill in the character chart.**

What Malka Is Like	Story Clues
Malka is brave.	*She travels to a new country alone.*

▶ **Use the story and your character chart to write the answers.**

1. How do you think the author wants the reader to feel about Malka? Explain.

2. Would you like to be friends with Malka? Tell why or why not.

Your Turn to Write

▶ **Think about someone you know who has reached an important goal or completed a difficult task. Use the character chart below to plan a story about him or her. Tell what the person is like and what he or she will do, say, think, and feel.**

What ______________ Is Like	Clues
____________________	____________________
____________________	____________________
____________________	____________________
____________________	____________________
____________________	____________________
____________________	____________________
____________________	____________________
____________________	____________________
____________________	____________________
____________________	____________________

▶ **On a separate sheet of paper, write a short story about the person you chose. Use the information from your character chart.**

LESSON 9

Pompeii: The City That Disappeared

What Do You Already Know?

What can natural disasters do to a town or city? What effects can nature have on our lives?

VOCABULARY

forum (FOR uhm) The town square of an ancient city

amphitheater (AM fuh THEE uh tuhr) A large outdoor semicircular arena

Get Ready to Read

A **cause** is the reason why something happens. An **effect** is what happens as a result. A cause can have more than one effect. As you read about the ancient city of Pompeii, look for cause-and-effect relationships.

Pompeii (pahm PAY) was once a beautiful city in ancient Italy. Pompeii was built more than 2500 years ago on a plateau of lava, nestled beside the Bay of Naples in Italy. Pompeii was located less than 1 mile (1.6 kilometers) south of the majestic Mount Vesuvius (vuh SOO vee uhs).

Pompeii was built in the shape of an oval. A great wall with eight gates encircled the city. It was a popular vacation area visited by wealthy people. At the center of the city was the **forum**, which was surrounded by many large public buildings. This included an **amphitheater** that could seat the entire population of Pompeii. The population was about 20,000 people.

Then one summer, this successful city was completely wiped out.

What Happened to Pompeii?

Mount Vesuvius, which looms in the background over Pompeii, proved to be the **demise** of the once thriving city. When the city was settled, Mount Vesuvius was a **dormant** volcano. It had not erupted for hundreds of years.

Seventeen years before Pompeii was wiped out, the town was struck by a massive earthquake. This earthquake could have set in motion the event that would eventually destroy the town. It is possible that this earthquake caused major Earth changes that would lead to the eruption of Mount Vesuvius. This, however, was not known by the citizens of Pompeii.

The citizens of Pompeii and nearby towns were in the middle of a regular day in August when **catastrophe** struck. Mount Vesuvius erupted suddenly and violently without any warning.

From the moment the eruptions began, the townspeople had only minutes to escape. People were forced to run for their lives without regard for their homes or property. They fled the area, chased by falling stones and clouds of ash.

Tip

An effect can have more than one cause. A cause can have more than one effect. Look for **multiple results** and **reasons** for causes and effects.

VOCABULARY

demise (dee MYZ) End

dormant (DOR muhnt) Inactive

catastrophe (kuh TASS truh fee) A terrible and sudden disaster

Clay containers like these were found in the ruins.

Tip

Clue words such as **because** and **reason** can help you find a cause. Clue words such as **so** and **result** can help you find an effect.

These murals were found unharmed in some of Pompeii's villas.

An Eyewitness to Disaster

Much of what we know of the disaster at Pompeii comes from a Roman writer named Pliny the Younger. Pliny the Younger was one of Pompeii's survivors. He wrote a letter that explained how he and his mother escaped to safety through the ash clouds and falling stones. Pliny wrote that the eruption lasted for four straight days. When it finally stopped, an estimated 2000 people were left buried under the ash and lava of the volcano.

In the **aftermath** of the eruption, only the tops of the city walls and columns rose above the waste. At first, survivors returned to try to dig out their valuables and belongings. However, later eruptions of Mount Vesuvius eventually buried the last traces of the city.

The eruption of Mount Vesuvius destroyed not only Pompeii, but other nearby cities and towns. In fact, because of the eruption, the whole geography of the area was changed. The eruption changed the path of the Sarno River. It also raised the beach that bordered the bay. As a result of these Earth changes, there was no longer any way of locating the city. Pompeii remained buried deep beneath many layers of ash for thousands of years.

VOCABULARY

aftermath
(AF tuhr math) The result of a disaster

A Window to the Past

An unbelievable discovery was made in 1748. One day, a farmer was digging in his vineyard located in the countryside of Italy. His shovel hit something hard. When he dug further, he discovered a wall. He had uncovered the long-buried city of Pompeii.

Pompeii's ruins are remarkably **intact**. This is a result of the showers of wet ashes and cinders that accompanied the eruption. These ashes and cinders formed an airtight seal. This **preserved** many structures.

As the ruins were carefully uncovered, the finest examples of ancient Roman art, buildings, and homes were revealed. In addition, the remains of some of the 2000 victims of the disaster were found in the ruins. Many victims were preserved in the same position they were in when Mount Vesuvius erupted.

Today, Pompeii is visited by many **archeologists**, as well as by tourists interested in history. The ruins provide a realistic picture of life in an ancient Italian city. Visitors are able to see the central forum and the public and private baths, typical of Roman towns. We know that Pompeii was a wealthy town because of the size of the homes. A typical **villa** had an average of forty rooms!

Archeologists are still working to uncover Pompeii piece by piece. They are preserving the details of Roman civilization for many generations to come.

This Basilica served as a courthouse, a temple, and the center of the town's government.

Tip

To find the cause, ask yourself, "**Why did this happen?**" To find the effect, ask yourself, "**What happened?**"

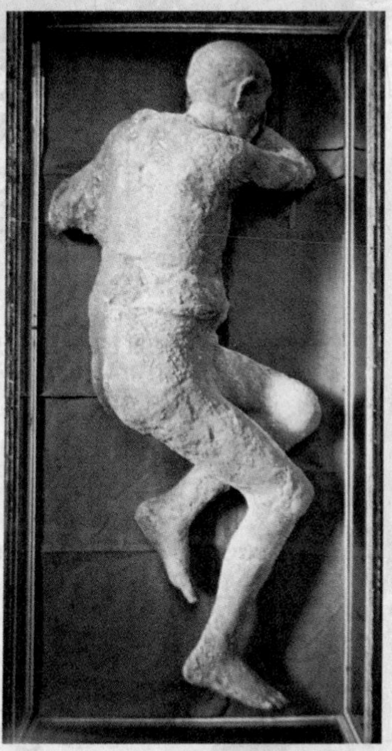

a preserved victim

VOCABULARY

intact (in TAKT) Not broken or harmed; complete

preserved (pree ZURVD) Kept safe or protected

archeologists (ar kee OL uh jists) People who dig up old buildings and objects to learn about the past

villa (VILL uh) A large, elaborate home

Comprehension Check

Circle the letter next to the best answer.

1. What is this article mostly about?

A. Vacation areas in Italy
B. The effects of a natural disaster
C. Careers in archeology
D. An ancient roman theater

2. Why were the people of Pompeii surprised by the eruption of Mount Vesuvius?

E. Because they lived in such a small town
F. Because the townspeople were wealthy
G. Because it had not erupted for hundreds of years
H. Because they thought it was an earthquake

3. The author most likely wrote this article to—

A. persuade tourists to visit the ruins at Pompeii
B. describe what an Italian city was like
C. explain a historical event in ancient Italy
D. analyze the art of the Roman Empire

4. Where does much of our knowledge about what happened to Pompeii come from?

E. The artifacts found at the site
F. The geography of the area
G. An eyewitness account
H. The farmer who dug up Pompeii

Answer the questions below in complete sentences.

5. What might it have been like to be in Pompeii when Mount Vesuvius erupted?

6. What can we learn from the discovery of the Pompeii ruins?

Vocabulary Builder

Write a word from the box to complete each sentence.

aftermath	**amphitheater**	**archeologists**
catastrophe	**forum**	**preserved**

1. The city of Pompeii had a ________________, or town square, where the townspeople went to shop and meet one another.
2. Citizens watched performances in the 20,000 seat ________________.
3. When Mount Vesuvius erupted, it was the worst ________________ the city had ever known.
4. In the ________________ of the eruption, survivors tried to dig out their belongings.
5. The ashes and cinders covered and ________________ many Pompeii buildings and homes for thousands of years.
6. From digging up ancient objects, ________________ have been able to learn about life in Pompeii.

EXTEND YOUR VOCABULARY

Synonyms **Synonyms are words that have the same or almost the same meanings.**

Match each word in the box with its synonym. Write each word on the correct line.

demise	**dormant**	**intact**	**villa**

7. inactive ________________
8. mansion ________________
9. end ________________
10. unharmed ________________

Focus Skill

Cause and Effect

A **cause** is why something happens. An **effect** is what happens as a result. A cause can have more than one effect.

Use the article to complete the cause-and-effect chart.

Cause	Effects
Mount Vesuvius erupted in the ancient city of Pompeii.	*People had to flee the city.*

Use the article and your cause-and-effect chart to answer the questions.

1. Why was the city of Pompeii buried for so long?

2. What things have happened as a result of the farmer digging in the field?

Your Turn to Write

Think about a natural disaster such as a hurricane, a tornado, or a blizzard. Use the cause-and-effect chart to list the cause and effects related to this natural disaster.

Cause	Effects
____________________	____________________
____________________	____________________
____________________	____________________
____________________	____________________
	____________________
	____________________
	____________________
	____________________

On a separate sheet of paper, write a short article about the natural disaster you chose. Use the information from your cause-and-effect chart to describe how this disaster is caused and what its effects can be.

LESSON 10

Creepy, Crawly . . . and Delicious: Insects as Food

What Do You Already Know?

What is the strangest food you have ever eaten? What did it look like? What did it taste like? Did you enjoy it?

Get Ready to Read

A **fact** is a statement that can be proven true. An **opinion** is someone's belief or feeling. As you read, try to decide what is a statement of fact and what is a statement of opinion.

Believe it or not, most insects we see crawling on the ground or on our picnic blankets can be eaten. In fact, many bugs and insects are quite **nutritious**. Insects are low in fat and are good sources of protein. Insects can also be quite tasty if they are cooked properly. Many cookbooks feature insect recipes. There are even **entomology** newsletters and magazines devoted to insects as food.

You may not like the idea of eating a grasshopper or a beetle. But insects are probably better for you than the high-fat, high-salt, high-calorie diet that many people have today. Put down the fast food and get ready to pass the pest food!

VOCABULARY

nutritious
(noo TRISH uhss) Good for the body

entomology
(en tuh MOL uh gee) The study of insects

Fried waterbugs might make a tasty appetizer.

What's That Fly Doing in My Soup?

Does the idea of eating creepy crawlers sound less than **appetizing** to you? Don't get scared, but did you ever notice tiny black specks in your cereal or bread? These might be flour beetles and other pests that live in **granaries**. They fall into the flour as the grain is being milled.

Did you ever notice tiny things flying around fruit in the market? Well, guess what they are? Fruit flies! Chances are you've been eating insects without even knowing it. Now that you have your feet wet, why don't you take the full plunge and taste a few delicious insect **morsels**?

If you'd like to try adding insects to your diet, it's important to know how to prepare them. What is the first step on the road to successful insect-eating? All insect food experts will tell you the same thing. Get the freshest insects you can find, and cook them before eating them.

Insects usually are not found in supermarkets. However, you can purchase insects in pet stores or bait stores. You can also catch insects in the wild.

Besides eating the whole insect, insect parts are also good to eat. You may want to begin by trying wings, legs, and eggs. Insects can make delicious main courses or make a lovely **garnish** for a festive holiday plate.

Tip

If you are not sure if something is a fact or an opinion, ask yourself, "Could this be **proven** true?" If so, then it is a statement of fact.

VOCABULARY

appetizing
(AP uh ty zing) Something that looks and smells good to eat

granaries
(GRAYN uh reez) Buildings for storing grain

morsels (MOR suhlz)
Small pieces of food

garnish (GAR nish)
A piece of food used as a decoration on a main dish

Enjoy crunchy beetles as a main course.

Tip

Think about why the author includes his or her opinions in an article. What is he or she trying to **persuade** you to think or believe?

International Insect Snacks

Eating insects is not a new trend. In fact, people have been eating insects throughout history. Native Americans ate plenty of different insects long before Christopher Columbus came to America.

Today, many cultures around the world have insects in their **cuisine**. In fact, eighty percent of the world's population eats insects. In South America, people eat white beetles and ants. In Mexico, there is a particular ant that people use to make salsa. This ant is found only during the rainy season. In Algeria, people collect locusts in the desert, cook them in salt water, and dry them in the sun before eating them. In Japan, many insect items can be found on restaurant menus, such as boiled wasp **larvae** and fried grasshoppers with rice. People in West Africa eat termites and caterpillars.

Insects are not only tasty and nutritious, they are also **plentiful**. Yet why aren't people in America eating more insects today? The answer is simple. Many people think that insects are disgusting! You might agree, but imagine you were lost in the woods and it was getting dark. If you had to choose between starving and eating insects, what would you do? Who knows? You might find the crispy crunch of roasted ants to be **irresistible**.

VOCABULARY

cuisine (kwi ZEEN) A style of cooking

larvae (LAR vy) Insects at the stage of development between egg and pupa

plentiful (PLEN ti fuhl) Existing in large amounts

irresistible (ir i ZISS tuh buhl) Too tempting to resist

Chocolate-covered insects could be a perfect after-school snack!

We're Having *What* for Breakfast?

Tired of the same old, boring pancakes? Here's a simple and delicious recipe for grasshopper cakes to start your day right!

Tip

Words such as **boring** and **delicious** can give clues about the author's opinion.

Grasshopper Cakes

- one egg
- twenty fresh, cooked grasshoppers
- two cups of cornmeal
- one teaspoon of cooking oil

1. Beat the egg in a bowl. Then add the grasshoppers and stir.
2. Put the grasshopper-and-egg mixture into a paper bag filled with cornmeal.
3. Make sure that the top of the bag is closed. Then shake the bag until the insects are completely covered with cornmeal.
4. Take the mixture out of the bag and make small pancake-size cakes, using your hands.
5. Ask an adult to help you fry the cakes in a skillet with a teaspoon of cooking oil. Drain and cool the cakes on a paper towel.
6. Serve plain or with syrup, butter, or honey.

Don't Let Insects Bug You!

Do you think you will be cooking buggy recipes anytime soon? If you do, remember that insects must be gathered and prepared properly. It's best to check with a health professional, a science teacher, or a parent before you take your first creepy, crawly, crunchy bite. Happy eating!

Comprehension Check

Answer the questions below in complete sentences.

1. What would be another good title for this article?

____

2. What is the second step in making grasshopper cakes?

____

____

3. Why do you think the author wrote this article?

____

____

4. Why might insects be better for you than some of the foods you might eat regularly?

____

____

5. According to this article, how do people in Mexico use a particular ant in their food?

____

____

6. Do you think it is a good idea to eat insects? Explain.

____

____

____

Vocabulary Builder

Circle the letter next to the best answer.

1. In this article, entomology means—
   - **A** the study of humans
   - **B** the study of insects
   - **C** the study of recipes
   - **D** the study of foods

2. In this article, nutritious means—
   - **E** unimportant
   - **F** good for the body
   - **G** delicious
   - **H** a type of insect

3. In this article, morsels means—
   - **A** large insects
   - **B** recipes
   - **C** small pieces of food
   - **D** small insects

4. In this article, garnish means—
   - **E** a main dish
   - **F** an insect from South America
   - **G** a small animal
   - **H** a piece of food used as a decoration

5. In this article, cuisine means—
   - **A** a chef
   - **B** a style of cooking
   - **C** a type of insect
   - **D** a pancake

6. In this article, larvae means—
   - **E** insect bites
   - **F** ingredients
   - **G** young insects
   - **H** insect recipes

EXTEND YOUR VOCABULARY

Root Words **Look for root words to help you understand the meanings of unfamiliar words.**

Draw lines between the two columns to match each root word with the correct vocabulary word. Then write the definition of each vocabulary word on the line next to it.

7. appetite •	• irresistible	____________________
8. grain •	• plentiful	____________________
9. resist •	• appetizing	____________________
10. plenty •	• granaries	____________________

Focus Skill

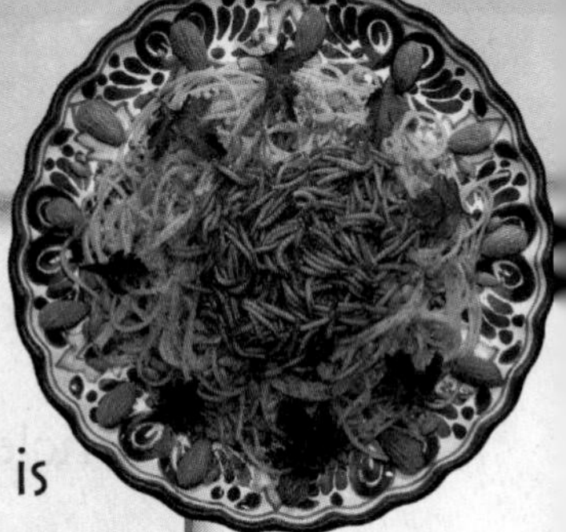

A **fact** is a statement that can be proven true. An **opinion** is someone's belief or feeling. A writer can give both facts and opinions in an article.

Use the article to fill in the fact-and-opinion chart. In the first column, write facts from the article. In the second column, write opinions from the article.

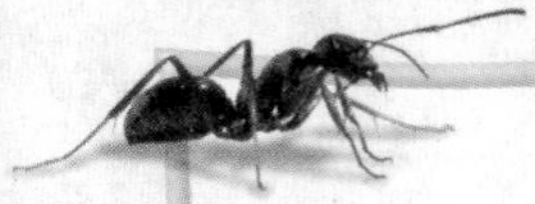

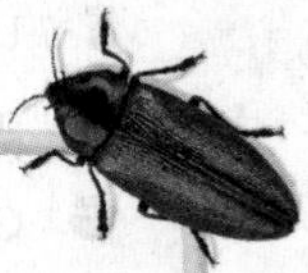

Facts	Opinions
Most insects can be eaten.	*Insect parts are also good to eat.*

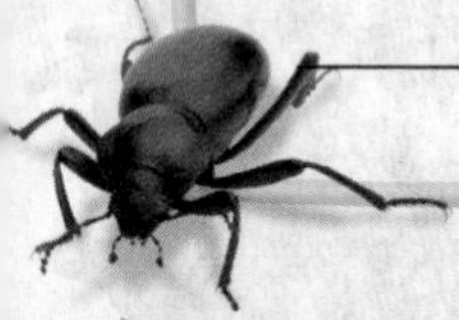

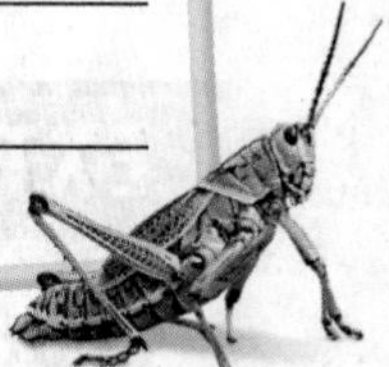

Use the article and your fact-and-opinion chart to write the answers.

1. How does the author feel about insects as food?

____

____

2. After reading the article, do you feel differently about eating insects? Explain.

____

____

____

Your Turn to Write

Choose an unusual kind of food that you know how to make or like to eat. How might you persuade readers to try this food? Use the fact-and-opinion chart below to list the facts and your opinions about the food.

I would like readers to try ______________________________.

Facts	Opinions

On a separate sheet of paper, write a short article to persuade readers to try the food you chose. Use the information from your fact-and-opinion chart.

LESSON 11

What Do You Already Know?

Think about a myth or fable that you have read. Did the story teach a lesson? What was it?

VOCABULARY

labyrinth (LAB uh rinth)
A complicated maze

intricate (IN tri kit)
Detailed and complicated

ensure (en SHOOR)
To make certain that something happens

THE STORY OF ICARUS: A GREEK MYTH

Get Ready to Read

The **theme** is the **moral**, or **lesson**, of a story. You can often find the theme of a story by looking for the lesson a character learns. As you read, look for the theme of this myth.

Daedalus (DEHD uh luhs) was a clever inventor who served King Minos on the Greek island of Crete. Daedalus invented and built many wonderful things for King Minos. Daedalus's son, Icarus (IK uh ruhs), was learning his father's trade and often worked by his side. However, Icarus had a bad habit of ignoring the things his father told him.

"Don't rush," Daedalus would tell his son. "Your work will be sloppy." But Icarus would not listen to his father, and Daedalus would have to undo his son's mistakes.

Among the things Daedalus created for King Minos was a **labyrinth**. It was an **intricate** maze that twisted and turned in many directions. The labyrinth was built to contain the fierce Minotaur (MIN uh taur), a beast that was half-man and half-bull. The king prized this beast and had Daedalus build the labyrinth to **ensure** that the beast would never escape.

One day a man named Theseus came to the island of Crete. Theseus was jealous of King Minos and wanted to make him angry. He was able to work his way into the labyrinth, and he killed the Minotaur. When Theseus fled, the king punished Daedalus **unjustly**. The labyrinth was supposed to have kept the Minotaur safe, and the king felt that Daedalus had failed him.

King Minos locked Daedalus and Icarus in the labyrinth. He told them they would be trapped in the labyrinth, and on the island, forever. Although Daedalus had built the maze himself and knew how to escape, the king's guards stood at the only exit. Icarus wanted to attack the guards and escape right away.

"You must learn to be patient, son," Daedalus told him. "The guards are armed. We would be killed. We must think of another plan."

That night as Icarus slept, Daedalus sat awake. When the sun rose and Daedalus watched the birds fly overhead, he had an idea. The only way to escape the labyrinth would be to fly through the air to get to the mainland of Greece.

The very next day and for many days after that, Daedalus led Icarus through the labyrinth. They both collected bird feathers and the drippings from the wax candles that lit the grand maze. Finally, it was time to set the plan into action.

Tip

Sometimes the theme is not stated in the story. You can figure out the theme from the **actions** of the characters and what happens at the end of the story.

VOCABULARY

unjustly (un JUST lee)
Not fairly

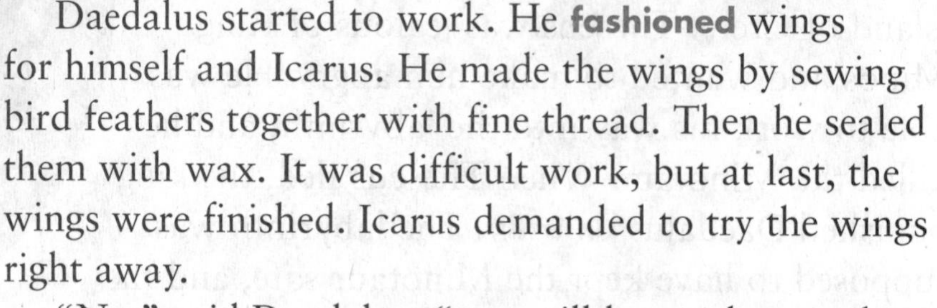

Tip

As you read, ask yourself, "What does the author want me to **learn** from this story?"

Daedalus started to work. He **fashioned** wings for himself and Icarus. He made the wings by sewing bird feathers together with fine thread. Then he sealed them with wax. It was difficult work, but at last, the wings were finished. Icarus demanded to try the wings right away.

"No," said Daedalus, "you will be careless, and you will ruin them. We must find a spot where we can catch a good wind that will carry us to safety."

Daedalus led Icarus up to the highest point of the labyrinth. There the father and son put on their wings. Before they took off, Daedalus gave his son a warning.

"Do not fly too close to the sun. The heat will melt the wax of your wings. Do not fly too close to the water. The dampness will weigh down your feathers. Be sure to keep a middle course. Follow me, and you will be safe."

Daedalus kissed his **beloved** son, and then the two soared into the sky. At first, Icarus **heeded** his father's warnings. But soon, the boy grew bored. He flapped his wings harder. The cool breeze felt wonderful on his face. The land and people below looked like no more than tiny specks. The thrill of flying was **exhilarating**, and soon Icarus had flown far ahead of his father.

"Icarus, you must slow down!" called Daedalus. "I warned you not to be foolish!"

VOCABULARY

fashioned (FASH uhnd) Made something

beloved (bi LUV id) Greatly loved or dear to someone

heeded (HEED id) Paid close attention to

exhilarating (eg ZIL uh rayt ing) Very exciting and thrilling

But Icarus ignored him. *Surely nothing bad could happen to me in this beautiful sky*, thought Icarus. He continued to soar among the soft, **billowing** clouds. The warm rays of the sun felt wonderful. He decided to see how high he could fly.

Icarus climbed higher and higher into the sky. He did not notice how hot the sun was getting. He flew so high that he did not hear his father's calls.

"Icarus! Do not fly so close to the sun!" Daedalus cried. But it was no use. No answer came back to him. Soon Icarus had flown so high, his father could no longer see him.

Icarus soared onward and upward. He was lost in the joy of flight. By the time he noticed that the wax of his wings had begun to soften, it was too late. The wings loosened completely, and down, down, down Icarus went. He flapped his wings wildly, but it was no use. He disappeared into the sea.

Daedalus looked down into the water. He saw a few feathers floating on the surface and knew his son's fate. Icarus was lost in the waters that would from then on bear his name—the Icarian Sea.

At last, Daedalus arrived safely on land. But for as long as he lived, he **lamented** his son's stubborn nature. Now Icarus was gone. It was all because he had been impatient and never learned to listen.

Tip

After you read, ask yourself, "What was the **moral** of the story?"

VOCABULARY

billowing (BIL oh ing)
Swelling or rising

lamented (luh MENT id)
Felt great sadness

Comprehension Check

Fill in the circle next to the best answer.

1. What happened after Theseus killed the Minotaur?

Ⓐ Daedalus and Icarus were locked in the labyrinth.
Ⓑ Daedalus built the labyrinth.
Ⓒ Icarus sewed a pair of wings.
Ⓓ King Minos thanked Daedalus.

2. Where is the island of Crete?

Ⓔ Italy
Ⓕ United States
Ⓖ Greece
Ⓗ Russia

3. Why did Daedalus tell Icarus not to fly too close to the sun?

Ⓐ Because he didn't want him to get a sunburn
Ⓑ Because the wax of his wings would melt
Ⓒ Because he wanted him to stay cool
Ⓓ Because he didn't want him to be good at flying

4. Why was Daedalus sad at the end of the story?

Ⓔ His wings didn't work.
Ⓕ He missed the Minotaur.
Ⓖ King Minos was angry at him.
Ⓗ His son never learned to be patient and listen.

Answer the questions below in complete sentences.

5. What is Icarus like? Describe him.

____

____

____

6. Why did Daedalus keep reminding his son to be patient and listen to his advice?

____

____

____

Vocabulary Builder

Choose words from the box to complete the paragraph. Write each word on the correct line.

beloved	billowing	ensure	fashioned	heeded	labyrinth

Daedalus was a great inventor who ________(1) many wonderful things. One of his greatest inventions was an elaborate maze called a ________(2). He built it to ________(3) that the king's prized beast would never escape. When the beast was killed, the king locked Daedalus and his ________(4) son, Icarus, in the maze. Daedalus built wings for himself and his son, and at last they escaped. As they soared among the ________(5) clouds, Daedalus warned his son not to fly too close to the sun. But Icarus never ________(6) his father's warning, and he fell into the sea.

EXTEND YOUR VOCABULARY

Antonyms **Antonyms are words that have opposite meanings.**

Match each word in the box with its antonym. Write each word on the correct line.

exhilarating	intricate	lamented	unjustly

7. simple ________

8. rejoiced ________

9. fairly ________

10. boring ________

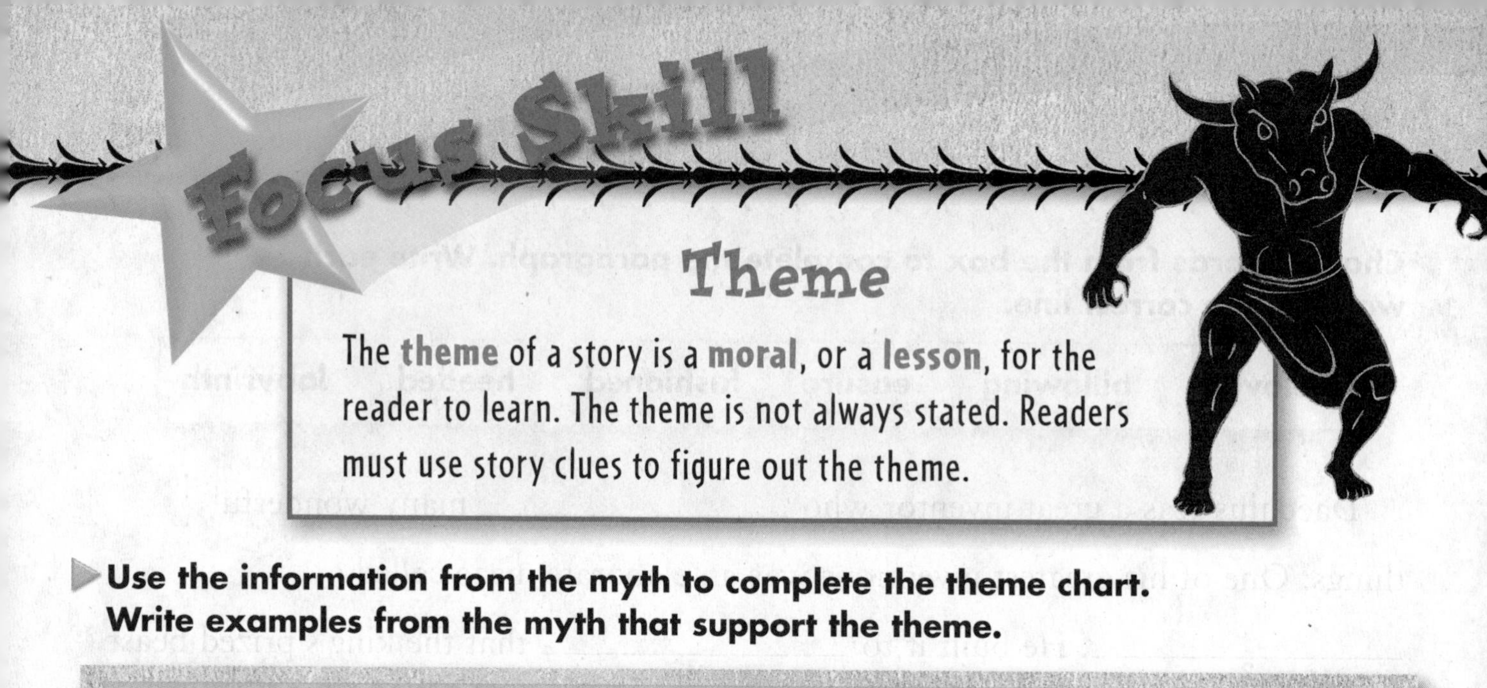

Theme

The **theme** of a story is a **moral**, or a **lesson**, for the reader to learn. The theme is not always stated. Readers must use story clues to figure out the theme.

Use the information from the myth to complete the theme chart. Write examples from the myth that support the theme.

THEME
____
____

EXAMPLES THAT SUPPORT THE THEME
Icarus did not listen to his father and made mistakes when he rushed through his work.
____
____
____

Use the myth and your theme chart to write the answers.

1. Why did Icarus ignore his father's warning?

____

____

2. What might have happened if Icarus had listened to his father?

____

____

____

Your Turn to Write

- Have you ever done something that you were sorry for later? What lesson did you learn? Use the theme chart below to plan a story about it.

THEME

EXAMPLES THAT SUPPORT THE THEME

- On a separate sheet of paper, write about what you did and the lesson you learned. Use the information from your theme chart.

LESSON 12

THE SEVEN WONDERS OF TODAY'S WORLD

What Do You Already Know?

If you were to make a list of seven places that you would like to visit, what places would you include? Why?

VOCABULARY

renowned (ri NOUND) Famous; well-known

compile (kuhm PYL) Put together

span (SPAN) Stretch across

Get Ready to Read

Text structure is the way a piece of writing is organized. Nonfiction may be organized different ways, such as in **chronological order**, by **topic**, by **cause and effect**, and by **comparison and contrast**. As you read, look for the text structure of this article.

The ancient Greeks and Romans made many different lists of man-made wonders of the world. Buildings and statues would qualify for the lists based on their size or another unusual quality. The most **renowned** list is now called the Seven Wonders of the Ancient World. All of those wonders were located in a small region around the Mediterranean Sea.

Today, many more amazing man-made wonders have been constructed all over the world. In the tradition of the Greeks and Romans, we can **compile** our own list of wonders that **span** the globe. These are wonders that we can visit today. Only one of the original seven ancient wonders still exists. A tour of today's wonders starts there, in the deserts of Egypt.

The Pyramids of Giza

The Great Pyramid of Giza

The pyramids of Egypt were tombs for **pharaohs**. The largest pyramid was built at Giza, for Pharaoh Kuhfu. When it was completed in 2580 B.C., it was the tallest structure in the world. It held that record for nearly 4000 years. It is made up of over two million blocks of heavy limestone and granite. How did the ancient Egyptians build this massive structure without machines? No one knows for sure. However, most experts think the blocks were hauled up sloping ramps with ropes. Visitors from all over the world still flock to see this ancient wonder today.

The Great Wall of China

The Great Wall of China snakes through the mountains of northern China for more than 1500 miles (2414 kilometers). If it were in the U.S., it would stretch from Washington, D.C. to Denver, Colorado. The Great Wall is so large that it can even be seen from space.

The Great Wall started in different places as protection for different states. The individual sections were connected during the Qin (CHIN) Dynasty from 221–206 B.C. This tradition of connecting the wall lasted for centuries. Each dynasty added to the wall's height, length, and design.

During the Ming dynasty, from 1368–1644, the wall took on its present form. The brick work was enlarged and **sophisticated** designs were added. Many parts of the wall have been destroyed over the years. However, much of the wall has been restored, so visitors can still see this achievement.

Tip

The **subheads** in an article can help you understand the structure of the text.

VOCABULARY

pharaohs (FAIR ohz)
Ancient kings of Egypt

sophisticated
(suh FISS tuh KAYT id)
Cleverly designed; complicated

The Great Wall of China

Tip

A **well-organized** article presents information in a logical order.

Machu Picchu

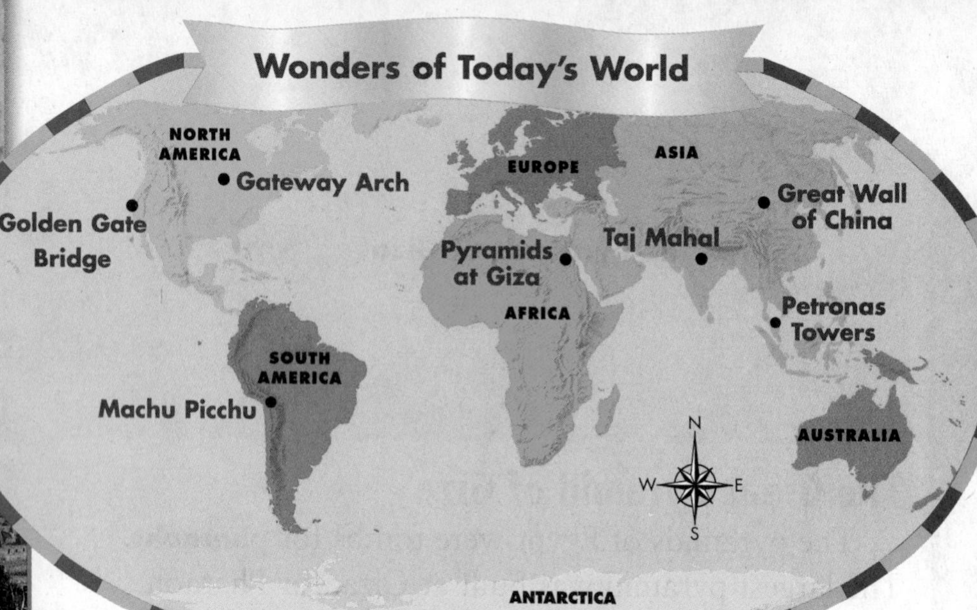

VOCABULARY

terraces (TER uh sez) Flat surfaces on a hill used for growing crops

mausoleum (maw suh LEE uhm) A large building that houses a tomb

symmetrical (si ME tri kuhl) Having matching points on both sides of a dividing line

Machu Picchu

Machu Picchu (MAH choo PEEK choo) is the site of an ancient Inca city located in Peru on a mountain top. This ancient city is hidden between two larger peaks. Built between 1460 and 1470, Machu Picchu was remarkably intact when it was discovered in 1911 by an American explorer. This ancient city consists of stone buildings, walls, towers, and **terraces**. Everything is linked by a network of 3000 steps. This ancient city was entirely self-contained. The people of Machu Picchu did not have to travel outside of the city to find food and water. The terraces grew enough food to feed the population and fresh water flowed from natural springs.

The Taj Mahal

Many people consider the Taj Mahal in India to be the world's most beautiful building. An Indian emperor built it between 1632 and 1648 as a monument to his dead wife. It is actually a **mausoleum** that houses her grave. This spectacular monument is built entirely of white marble. **Symmetrical** towers frame the main building. Part of the monument's beauty is that it seems to change color. At dawn, it can appear pink. At night, it seems to glow in the moonlight.

Taj Mahal

The Golden Gate Bridge

The Golden Gate Bridge, located in San Francisco, California, has been **heralded** as one of the top construction achievements of the twentieth century. The height of the towers reaches 746 feet (227 meters) above the water of the Golden Gate Strait. The total length of the bridge spans 8981 feet (2737 meters). The Golden Gate Bridge is known as one of the world's most beautiful bridges. It has tremendous towers, sweeping cables, and brilliant color. The bridge was ready for cars in 1938.

Tip

Reviewing the **subheads** is a good study aid after you have read an article.

The Golden Gate Bridge

The Gateway Arch

Soaring 630 feet (192 meters) above the Mississippi River, the Gateway Arch in Saint Louis, Missouri is America's tallest human-made monument. The Gateway Arch is a memorial to Thomas Jefferson and to the historic role Saint Louis played as the gateway to the west. The construction of this astounding stainless steel arch was completed in 1965.

The Gateway Arch

VOCABULARY

heralded (HER uhl duhd) Proclaimed; announced

spires (SPYRZ) Structures that come to a point at the top

Petronas Twin Towers

Until 1998, the world's tallest skyscraper had always been in the United States. But that year, the Petronas Twin Towers in Kuala Lumpur, Malaysia, squeaked past Chicago's Sears Tower by 33 feet (10 meters). The **spires** on top of the Petronas Towers peak at an impressive 1483 feet (452 meters). The identical towers are linked by a bridge which creates a dramatic gateway to Kuala Lumpur. Other features of these towers include a curtain wall of glass and stainless steel sun shades. The shades are important because Malaysia is close to the equator where the sun's rays are the strongest.

Petronas Twin Towers

Comprehension Check

Answer the questions below in complete sentences.

1. Why do you think the author selected these particular structures to write about?

____

____

2. Why was the Great Wall of China built?

____

____

____

3. How are the Pyramid at Giza and the Taj Mahal alike? How are they different?

____

____

____

4. Why was the Gateway Arch built?

____

____

5. Why is it necessary for the Petronas Twin Towers to have sun shades?

____

____

6. Which of these wonders would you most like to see? Tell why.

____

____

____

Vocabulary Builder

Fill in the circle next to the best answer.

1. In this article, compile means—

Ⓐ put together
Ⓑ take apart
Ⓒ take down
Ⓓ put away

2. In this article, span means—

Ⓔ far away
Ⓕ leave behind
Ⓖ bring together
Ⓗ stretch across

3. In this article, sophisticated means—

Ⓐ simply designed; plain
Ⓑ cleverly designed; complicated
Ⓒ incredibly large; massive
Ⓓ extremely ugly; offensive

4. In this article, heralded means—

Ⓔ listened; heard
Ⓕ scolded; warned
Ⓖ proclaimed; announced
Ⓗ wished; hoped

5. In this article, spires means—

Ⓐ bridges that span long distances
Ⓑ monuments to honor royalty
Ⓒ structures that come to a point
Ⓓ tombs that house ancient rulers

6. In this article, terraces means—

Ⓔ several houses on a hill
Ⓕ flat surfaces on a hill used for growing crops
Ⓖ natural springs with fresh water
Ⓗ large fields on flat ground

EXTEND YOUR VOCABULARY

Analogies **Analogies are pairs of words that have the same relationship.**

Complete each analogy with a word from the box.

mausoleum	**pharaohs**	**renowned**	**symmetrical**

7. *Unpopular* is to *popular* as *unknown* is to ________________.

8. *Book* is to *library* as *tomb* is to ________________.

9. *Unbalanced* is to *balanced* as *uneven* is to ________________.

10. *United States* is to *presidents* as *Ancient Egypt* is to ________________.

Text Structure

Text structure is the way an article is organized.

Write the oldest five wonders in order from oldest to most recent.

NAME OF WONDER	WHERE IT IS LOCATED	WHAT MAKES IT A WONDER
The Great Pyramid of Giza	*Egypt*	*It was the tallest structure in the world for nearly 4000 years.*

Use the article and your text structure chart to answer the questions.

1. How did the subheads in this article help you?

____

2. What might be another way the author could have organized this article?

____

Your Turn to Write

Think about other amazing buildings, bridges, or monuments that you know. Pick three that would be good choices for a top ten list of wonders of the world. Fill in the text structure chart with information about your own choices.

NAME OF WONDER	WHERE IT IS LOCATED	WHAT MAKES IT A WONDER

On another sheet of paper, write a short article that explains your choices. Use words to persuade your readers that your choices are world wonders. Use your text structure chart to help you.

REVIEW

▶ **Read the article. Then answer the questions.**

Steven Spielberg—Boy Wonder

Do you want to be a successful movie director like Steven Spielberg? You'd better get started—now! The Oscar-winning creator of such fantastic movies as *Jaws*, *E.T.*, *Saving Private Ryan*, and *Jurassic Park* was charging admission to his homemade movies when he was just twelve. According to one viewer, the young Spielberg's movies were full of clever techniques.

Childhood memories echo throughout Spielberg's thoughts and his movies. He remembers seeing a movie about Davy Crockett when he was eight. Davy said, "Be sure you're right, and then go ahead." This became Spielberg's motto. He's never stopped working to turn his dreams into successful realities.

Spielberg also remembers when his father took him to see a meteor shower. At first, young Steven was scared to be wakened in the middle of the night. Then the beautiful lights enchanted him. The mystery of outer space became something Steven wanted to explore.

Not all of Steven Spielberg's childhood was happy. Steven's family moved frequently, and his parents divorced. Some of his films feature a lonely or scared child seeking comfort or safety. Yet his films also express the joy and wonder of childhood. Like all great artists, Spielberg draws on his personal experiences. The grown man who made the movie called *E.T.: The Extra-Terrestrial* was once a boy who missed his father and loved the mystery of outer space.

Circle the letter next to the best answer.

1. Which fact would be least important to include in a summary?
   - **A.** Young Steven was scared when his father wakened him to watch a meteor shower.
   - **B.** Steven wanted to explore the mystery of outer space.
   - **C.** Steven has directed films such as *E.T.* and *Jurassic Park*.
   - **D.** Not all of Steven Spielberg's childhood was happy.

2. Which of the following statements is a fact?
   - **E.** Young Spielberg's movies were full of clever techniques.
   - **F.** The meteor shower was beautiful.
   - **G.** Steven's family moved frequently.
   - **H.** Steven Spielberg is a great artist.

3. Which best explains what motivates Steven to be a success?
   - **A.** He saw a movie about Davy Crockett when he was eight.
   - **B.** He has made Oscar-winning movies.
   - **C.** His motto is "Be sure you're right, then go ahead."
   - **D.** He wanted to explore the mysteries of outer space.

4. What is the theme of this article?
   - **E.** Davy Crockett was a great hero.
   - **F.** Steven Spielberg was a sad and lonely child.
   - **G.** You should be a director like Steven Spielberg.
   - **H.** Childhood was important to Steven Spielberg's career.

Answer the questions below in complete sentences.

5. What kind of person is Steven Spielberg? How can you tell?

6. What is the third paragraph mainly about?

7. What lesson can you learn from Steven Spielberg?

Read the story. Then answer the questions.

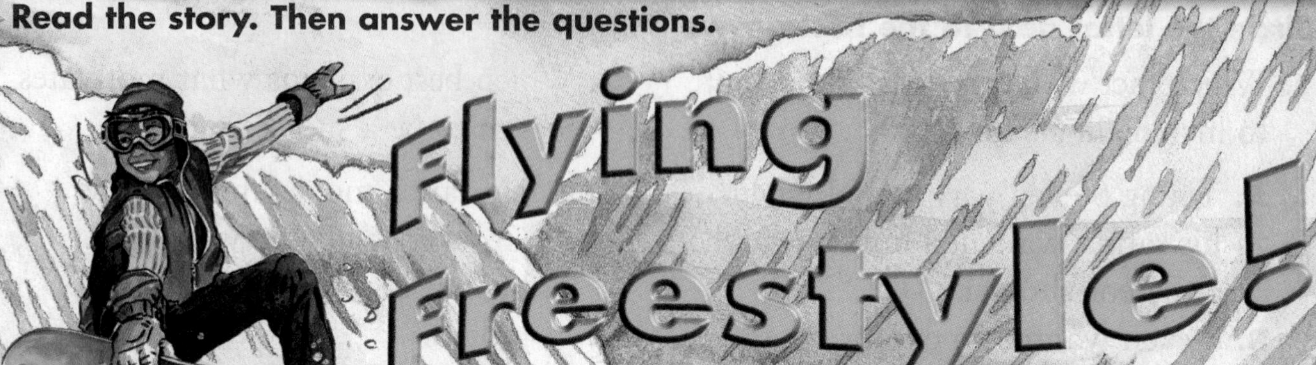

Flying Freestyle!

Kevin glided smoothly off the chairlift and headed down the mountain, gracefully bending his knees. Today he would be riding the pipe, a long gulley cut into the snow. His heart was beating fast, but his mind was clear. He would do two tricks. First a grab, and second, straight air. He believed he could win his first snowboarding competition. Kevin felt totally confident.

As he waited for his turn, Kevin remembered learning to snowboard. First, he had fallen off the chairlift and had to scramble out of the way of the riders behind him. Then he kept leaning back on his board instead of forward, which made him fall every time. Still, Kevin had refused to give up, and now he was competing!

The rider before Kevin was last year's champion. He dropped into the pipe awkwardly, and by the end of his run he was clearly off-balance. The judges took off points for his sketchy trick.

Then it was Kevin's turn. He took a deep breath and began swooshing back and forth down the pipe. He flew up into the air, grabbed his board for a second, and landed back in the pipe—perfect. On his next run, Kevin sailed straight up into the air, turned 180 degrees, and made another perfect landing.

Applause broke out before he reached the bottom of the mountain, but it wasn't until he saw his dad jumping up and down and yelling, "Number One!" that he finally relaxed. He had taken first place!

Circle the letter next to the best answer.

1. Which paragraph describes events that took place earlier than the rest of the story?

A Paragraph 1
B Paragraph 2
C Paragraph 3
D Paragraph 4

2. Which statement is an opinion?

E Kevin was gracefully bending his knees.
F The pipe was a long gulley cut in the snow.
G First he had fallen off the chair.
H He flew up into the air and grabbed his board.

3. Why didn't last year's champion win this year?

A He fell getting off the chairlift.
B He leaned back on his board.
C He was off-balance at the end of his run.
D He grabbed his board.

4. Kevin relaxed when he—

E got off the chairlift smoothly
F watched the rider before him
G heard applause
H saw his dad

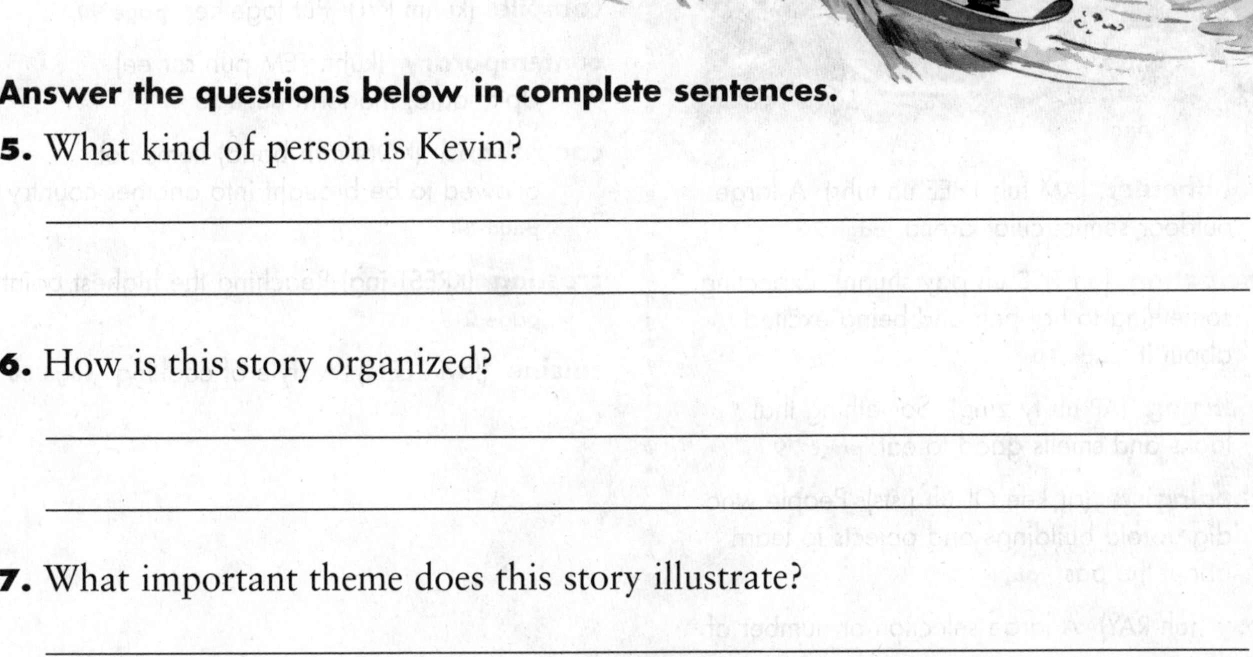

Answer the questions below in complete sentences.

5. What kind of person is Kevin?

____

____

6. How is this story organized?

____

____

7. What important theme does this story illustrate?

____

____

Glossary

A

accelerate (ak SEL uhr ayt) Go faster and faster **page 28**

accessible (ak SESS uh buhl) Reachable **page 35**

accumulated (uh KYOOM yoo lay ted) Collected; piled up **page 37**

adjacent (uh JAY suhnt) Close to or next to **page 36**

adorn (uh DORN) Decorate **page 37**

adrift (uh DRIFT) Drifting or floating freely through water or air **page 19**

aftermath (AF tuhr math) The result of a disaster **page 72**

amphitheater (AM fuh THEE uh tuhr) A large outdoor semicircular arena **page 70**

anticipation (an TISS uh pay shuhn) Expecting something to happen and being excited about it **page 10**

appetizing (AP uh ty zing) Something that looks and smells good to eat **page 79**

archeologists (ar kee OL uh jists) People who dig up old buildings and objects to learn about the past **page 73**

array (uh RAY) A large selection or number of things **page 3**

B

beloved (bi LUV id) Greatly loved or dear to someone **page 88**

billowing (BIL oh ing) Swelling or rising **page 89**

breakthrough (BRAYK throo) An important step toward achieving something **page 65**

breathtaking (BRETH tayk ing) Very beautiful or impressive **page 62**

buoyancy (BOI uhn see) Ability to float **page 43**

C

careening (kuh REEN ing) Swaying from side to side while moving quickly; lurching **page 29**

catastrophe (kuh TASS truh fee) A terrible and sudden disaster **page 71**

circuit (SUR kit) A group of related events that people attend **page 3**

collaboration (kuh LAB uh RAY shuhn) Working together to do something **page 56**

compile (kuhm PYL) Put together **page 94**

contemporary (kuhn TEM puh rer ee) Up-to-date; modern **page 55**

contraband (KON truh band) Items not allowed to be brought into another country **page 64**

cresting (KREST ing) Reaching the highest point **page 2**

cuisine (kwi ZEEN) A style of cooking **page 80**

D

debris (duh BREE) The scattered pieces of something; rubbish **page 29**

demise (dee MYZ) End **page 71**

demolish (di MOL ish) To destroy; defeat badly **page 27**

distribution (diss tri BYOO shuhn) The separation of things among people and places **page 42**

dormant (DOR muhnt) Inactive **page 71**

douse (DOUS) Wet thoroughly **page 42**

drowsy (DROU zee) Sleepy **page 13**

E

ejected (ee JEK tuhd) Pushed out **page 28**

elapsed (ee LAPSD) Passed, usually referring to time **page 34**

eliminate (ee LIM uh nayt) Get rid of **page 4**

embraced (em BRAYSSD) Clasped; hugged **page 45**

enclosure (en KLOH zuhr) An area closed off by walls **page 27**

encounter (en KOUN tuhr) Meet, especially in a dangerous way **page 18**

endanger (en DAYN juhr) To threaten or put in a dangerous situation **page 44**

ensure (en SHOOR) To make certain that something happens **page 86**

entomology (en tuh MOL uh gee) The study of insects **page 78**

envelop (en VEL uhp) To cover or surround something completely **page 2**

evade (ee VAYD) To keep out of something's way; to avoid **page 19**

exhibited (eg ZIB it uhd) Shown to the public **page 54**

exhilarating (eg ZIL uh rayt ing) Very exciting and thrilling **page 88**

extinct (ek STINGKT) No longer living or existing **page 21**

extraordinary (ek STROR duh NER ee) Very unusual or remarkable **page 13**

fashioned (FASH uhnd) Made something **page 88**

forum (FOR uhm) The town square of an ancient city **page 70**

fossils (FOSS uhls) Remains or traces of plants or animals from the past **page 21**

frantically (FRAN tik lee) Excitedly **page 44**

G

gangplank (GANG plangk) A short bridge used for walking onto and off a ship **page 62**

garnish (GAR nish) A piece of food used as a decoration on a main dish **page 79**

granaries (GRAYN uh reez) Buildings for storing grain **page 79**

H

hatchlings (HACH lings) Baby animals that have come from eggs **page 18**

hazards (HAZ uhrds) Dangers or risks **page 18**

heeded (HEED id) Paid close attention to **page 88**

heralded (HER uhl duhd) Proclaimed; announced **page 97**

hoarse (HORSS) Having a rough or husky voice **page 13**

identical (eye DEN ti kuhl) Exactly alike **page 26**

identity (eye DEN tuh tee) Who a person is **page 4**

immigration (IM uh gray shuhn) Entry into a new country to live **page 63**

impact (IM pakt) The striking of one thing against another **page 44**

incompetent (in KOM puh tuhnt) Not very skilled at something **page 43**

inspired (in SPY urd) To be filled with excitement or ideas about something **page 56**

intact (in TAKT) Not broken or harmed; complete **page 73**

intricate (IN tri kit) Detailed and complicated **page 86**

intriguing (in TREEG ing) Fascinating; interesting **page 34**

irresistible (ir i ZISS tuh buhl) Too tempting to resist **page 80**

labyrinth (LAB uh rinth) A complicated maze **page 86**

lamented (luh MENT id) Felt great sadness **page 89**

larvae (LAR vy) Insects at the stage of development between egg and pupa **page 80**

maneuver (muh NOO vuhr) To move or steer something carefully into a particular position **page 2**

mausoleum (maw suh LEE uhm) A large building that houses a tomb **page 96**

media (MEE dee uh) Ways of expressing or carrying information to people **page 55**

minimum (MIN i muhm) The smallest possible amount **page 37**

molten (MOHLT uhn) Melted by heat **page 36**

morsels (MOR suhlz) Small pieces of food **page 79**

navigate (NAV uh gayt) To find one's way on or across **page 20**

nutritious (noo TRISH uhss) Good for the body **page 78**

oblong (ob LAWNG) Having an elongated shape **page 20**

outraged (OUT rayjd) Extremely angered **page 29**

overcome (oh vuhr KUM) To be strongly affected by something **page 63**

passage (PASS ij) A journey by ship **page 63**

persevered (pur suh VEERD) Did not give up, even when faced with difficulties **page 65**

persistence (puhr SIST uhns) Ability and willingness to keep going in spite of challenges **page 19**

pharaohs (FAIR ohz) Ancient kings of Egypt **page 95**

photogenic (foht uh JEN ik) To look very good in photographs **page 56**

plentiful (PLEN ti fuhl) Existing in large amounts **page 80**

precipice (PRES uh pis) A steep cliff **page 45**

precise (pree SYSS) Very accurate or exact **page 5**

preserved (pree ZURVD) Kept safe or protected **page 73**

professor (proh FESS uhr) A teacher of the highest rank at a college or university **page 55**

prolonging (proh LAWNG ing) Making something last longer **page 3**

refresh (ri FRESH) To feel fresh and strong again **page 11**

reluctant (ri LUK tuhnt) To be nervous about; to not want to do something **page 56**

renowned (ri NOUND) Famous; well-known **page 94**

resides (ri ZYDZ) lives **page 57**

resourceful (ri SORSS fuhl) Knowing how to do what is needed to solve problems **page 12**

retorted (ri TORT ed) Answered quickly and strongly **page 11**

S

scorching (SKORCH ing) Extremely hot **page 35**

seamstress (SEEM striss) A woman who sews for a living **page 63**

sinister (SIN is tuhr) Evil and threatening **page 26**

sophisticated (suh FISS tuh KAYT id) Cleverly designed; complicated **page 95**

span (SPAN) Stretch across **page 94**

sparse (SPARSS) Thinly spread **page 35**

spires (SPYRZ) Structures that come to a point at the top **page 97**

startled (STAR tuhld) Surprised or frightened **page 26**

strenuous (STREN yoo uhs) Needing great energy or effort **page 10**

surveying (SUHR vay ing) Looking at a whole scene or situation **page 12**

survival (suhr VY vuhl) Staying alive **page 11**

symbolized (SIM buh lyzd) Stood for **page 62**

symmetrical (si ME tri kuhl) Having matching points on both sides of a dividing line **page 96**

T

teetering (TEE tuhr ing) Unstable **page 45**

terraces (TER uh sez) Flat surfaces on a hill used for growing crops **page 96**

transformed (trans FORMD) Made a great change **page 5**

U

unjustly (un JUST lee) Not fairly **page 87**

V

villa (VILL uh) A large, elaborate home **page 73**

W

willingly (WILL ing lee) Ready and eager to help or do what is asked **page 57**